"The wisdom in this book is more than the story of Galen's continuation. It shines with truths that can help we, the living, find ourselves. From the other side come truths about the nature and purpose of being human and ultimately about the spirit of love. I believe completely in this book, as well as in the vital message that we on earth are so believed in."

—Cyndi Dale
The Subtle Body and *The Complete Book of Chakra Healing*

"The prose—at the sentence level, where readers really live—feels like a sturdy and beautiful bridge from mind to mind. Fine work. Thank you for your part in helping our evolving consciousness return to wholeness."

—Chris Kelly
Artist

"Dr. Raymond Moody talks about the afterlife. Dr. Melvin Morse was enlightened by children's miraculous experiences. Betty Eadie and many others experienced their own miracles. Now we have Galen's miraculous journey, with its own depth and insight. Galen will confirm and give much hope to those who need to hear his messages and experiences."

—L. S. Sanchez
Educator and child advocate

"In his life on this planet, Galen intuitively communicated with dogs in rare and joyful 'cross species' dialogue. It makes perfect sense that he would continue to communicate across other borders with spirits that he loves. *My Life after Life* confirms access to the gift some people realize they have been given."

—Carolyn Clark Beedle
Executive Director
Assistance Dogs of the West

"When I read this book I felt like I was meeting Galen. His obser-vatuions and use of language are engaging and delightful. (What a great kid!) There are gems of wisdom in *My Life after Life*. The more the reader knows, the more he or she will see in this book. It should be kept and reread from time to time."

—**Gretchen Vogel**
Author of *Choices in the Afterlife*

"I am deeply touched and mystified by the story. Such tragedy eventually offering comfort indicates that we are truly spiritual beings having a terrestrial existence. This supernatural and visionary book proves that genuine relationships never end."

—**Akiane Kramarik**
Artist and poet

my life after life

a posthumous memoir

GALEN STOLLER
(1991–2007)

Edited by K Paul Stoller, MD
Foreword by Bernie Siegel, MD

Dream Treader Press
Santa Fe, New Mexico

Published by: Dream Treader Press
404 Brunn School Road #D
Santa Fe, NM 87505
www.dreamtreaderpress.com
www.my-life-after-life.com

Book design and production: Janice St. Marie

First Edition
Copyright © 2011 by K Paul Stoller

A portion of the proceeds from the sale of this book will be donated to organizations around the world dedicated to the sustainability of assistance and search & rescue dogs.

Printed in the United States of America

Publisher's Cataloging-in-Publication Data
Stoller, Galen, 1991-2007 (Spirit)
    My life after life : a posthumous memoir / Galen Stoller; edited by K
    Paul Stoller. -- Santa Fe, N.M. : Dream Treader Press, c2011.
      p. ; cm.
      ISBN: 978-0-615-38307-1
      1. Stoller, Galen, 1991-2007. 2. Future life. 3. Spiritualism.
      4. Parapsychology. 5. Children--Death--Psychological aspects.
      6. Spiritualists--Biography. 7. Guides (Spiritualism). I. Stoller,
      K Paul. II. Title.

BF1311.F8 G35   2011 2010931180
133.901/3--dc22 1103

1 3 5 7 9 10 8 6 4 2

To my grandmother~
the last person on earth to give me a word of wisdom

CONTENTS

Foreword

I wanted to write a foreword to this book so that my words, combined with its content, might help open the reader's mind to the nature of life and death and the potential spectrum of experiences available to us all. After becoming a physician, I found I had received a great deal of medical information during my training but no real education about life and people. Therefore, when a patient asked for help in learning how to live between office visits and when I started counseling patients with life-threatening illnesses I could not deny my own experiences. Rather than close my eyes and reply, "I cannot accept what you are saying," I began to live my personal experiences and let them create my beliefs. I also did not worry about what other people thought of me, which freed me up to explore the nature of life and still be accepted among those important to me.

Perhaps I have never been normal. My open minded disposition first became apparent when I was four years old. I had taken a toy apart and put all the small pieces in my mouth, imitating workmen I'd seen who placed nails in their mouths before hammering them into wood. Suddenly I aspirated the pieces and began choking—a painful and unpleasant way to die. Then the struggle stopped, and I realized I was no longer in my body but looking down at a dying child with whom I no longer identified and wondering, much as a blind person can wonder how they see while having a near-death experience. I remember choosing death over life and, while being sucked back into the boy's body as his terminal vomiting dislodged the pieces, like a Heimlich maneuver allowing him to breathe, calling out, "Who did that?" I was quite angry about my choice not being respected. It gave me a sense that I wasn't in charge of the schedule.

Years later, as a busy doctor, I was involved in many people's lives and teaching around the world. When a friend phoned me and asked, "Why are you living this life?" I went into a trance and had a past-life experience in which I saw myself with a sword in hand killing living beings of every species. I killed out of fear of what my Lord would do to me if I questioned his judgment or ignored his requests. This emotional experience taught me about the importance of choosing the right Lord to follow. I now believe we are all impregnated with and affected by the consciousness that preceded us, like my becoming a surgeon so I could use a knife to cure instead of kill.

Additional events occurred while I was counseling people with life-threatening illnesses. One of my patients revealed to me that she was a mystic who communicated with the dead and had messages for me. Her messages, relating to people's names and manner of speech, were undeniably true. Since then, the dead have spoken to me and I have heard voices from the collective consciousness leading me to do meaningful things.

For example, while out walking on the morning of the day my father was going to die I heard a voice ask me how my parents met. I said I didn't know, and the voice replied, "Then ask your mother when you get to the hospital." I did, whereupon she started telling stories. Apparently my dad lost a coin toss and had to take my mother out on their first date. That and other disastrous stories created an environment in which my dad could die laughing.

On another occasion, when I had just finished writing a book entitled *Buddy's Candle*, about a dog and a child with cancer, I heard a voice tell me to go to the local animal shelter. When I entered the shelter and spotted a dog sitting beside the door, I asked, "What's his name?" "Buddy," I was told. "He's been here less than fifteen minutes." I explained I was there to take him home, which I promptly did. Our property was a rescue site for animals of many species, and our five children helped me care for them. I continue to rescue creatures, probably to make up for the killing I am aware of from my past life.

A further example of receiving good advice from voices emerging out of the collective consciousness occurred in an operating room, when my patient's heart stopped beating and he could not be resuscitated. Figuring I had nothing to lose, I did as instructed and said his name out loud, followed by, "It's not your time yet. Come on back." Immediately his heart started beating again, and he recovered.

Comedian Lily Tomlin says, "If you speak to God, it is called prayer. When God speaks to you, it is called schizophrenia." Knowing some people can't accept the healthy existence of voices, you may want to be careful who you share your voice's messages with, a precaution not taken in *My Life after Life*, in which a father records the words of his deceased son for whomever his readers may be. It takes courage to share the experiences that led to the writing of this book—and its foreword. Yet that is just what is needed for us all to benefit from the information.

Reports of continuing contact with deceased children is nothing new. When in safe surroundings, parents whose children have died will share mystical experiences indicating ongoing communication with them. Birds have flown in the window of our meeting room when a mother talked about her murdered daughter's love of birds; an exotic butterfly from South America appeared in the backyard of a family from Connecticut whose deceased son collected butterflies; a mother driving through a blizzard heard her child's voice tell her to slow down as she rounded a curve in the road, which saved her from crashing into a pileup of cars. I used to wonder why these children were still communicating years after they had died. Why weren't they back in another body and not wasting time? I remained puzzled until I saw the show *Carousel*, in which a man dies while his daughter is an infant, so when an angel asks him if he wants to see her graduate from school he says she is an infant, and the angel responds, "There's no time up here."

Playwrights, poets, and creative authors are messengers aware of life's subtle truths. So when they speak from their experience, we can accept and believe. From the pages of this book, for instance, you will learn that consciousness is nonlocal and its existence does not require a physical body; nor is there separation involved in consciousness. I know from my work with dreams, drawings, and communicating with people and animals that consciousness is not limited and can be used for relaying information. If we are distraught about our loss, locked in grief and fear, or preoccupied with other thoughts, the mind will be too agitated to receive messages. The quiet mind, however, often symbolized in myths and religions by a still pond, allows us to see our true selves in its reflection. With a quiet mind we become open to perceiving the truth and experiencing life as it actually is—at which point, theory and reality can exist together.

Here a father listens intently to the words of his deceased son. As Swiss psychiatrist Carl Jung says in *Jung on Death and Immortality*: "You need not be insane to hear [such a] voice. On the contrary, it is the simplest and most natural thing imaginable. For instance, you can ask yourself a question to which 'he' gives answer." I have found you can converse with a friend of your soul, or your inner guide, by asking questions of him.

I can remember trying to share my experience through articles to medical journals, and they were returned with a note saying, "Interesting but inappropriate." When I sent them to psychology journals, they were returned with a note stating, "Appropriate but not interesting." That is when my anger at the lack of a true medical education began to surface. Our literature limits us to the technology involved in our particular specialty. We diagnose and prescribe, but do not listen and learn about the patient's experience. We have to stop focusing on theories and look at the true reality of life and death. It is all about beginnings, just as a graduation is called a commencement and the Bible ends in a revelation and not a conclusion.

In fact, according to Jung, "the future is unconsciously prepared long in advance and, therefore, can be guessed by clairvoyants." And when you leave your body, as author William Saroyan writes, you become "dreamless, unalive, perfect." Each life is like a candle the length of which has nothing to do with one's age but with how much time one has left to live until their candle burns out.

Too many people burn out ahead of time because they lose themselves attempting to become what others want them to be. Others fail to eliminate what is killing them and hence kill themselves and others out of revenge for prior rejection or abuse. We all need to listen to our hearts and not our heads. Even so, we do not have a perfect world because perfection is not creation; it is a magic trick. We are here to learn from the wisdom of those who have preceded us. And the wisdom of the dead, like the survival themes of religions and the works of great philosophers, urges us to pay attention and live the longest, healthiest lives we are capable of living. In raising our level of consciousness, we can then provide wisdom to future generations. In other words, when we learn how to heal our lives the world itself will be healed through our consciousness.

Even so, death is not the worst outcome. Henry Thomas, in his book *Understanding the Great Philosophers,* writes: "All civilization is nothing but an evolutionary process which enables man to adapt himself to an inhospitable world and to survive for a brief space in the eternal struggle for existence. For all life is a continual warfare, and there is no truce for any of us except in death." In using the pains of our struggle as labor pains, we have a chance to give birth to a new self with a higher level of consciousness. And with death comes the knowledge of how to make our future life complete.

Spiritual teacher Eknath Easwaren says, "No matter how hard we may try, in the long run none of us can escape the devastating fact of death. Yet an encounter with death can leave us changed decidedly for the better. It can prompt us forward on the long search for something secure in life, something death cannot reach." What is secure, permanent, and immortal is love. Love is the bridge between the living and the dead. This is the message we continually receive from the dead.

As you read on and learn from the wisdom communicated in this book, remember the poignant words of Helen Keller: "The inner or mystic sense gives me vision of the unseen. They skeptically declare that I see light that never was. But I know that their mystic sense is dormant, and that is why there are so many barren places in their lives. They prefer facts to vision. They want a scientific demonstration and they can have it. It is out of this ape that God creates the seer, and science meets spirit as life meets death, and life and death are one."

—BERNIE SIEGEL, MD

Editor's Note to the Reader

It would be frivolous of me to try to conceal from the reader
that such reflections are not only exceedingly unpopular but even
come perilously close to those turbid fantasies which becloud the minds
of world-reformers and other interpreters of "signs and portents."
But I must take this risk, even if it means putting my hard-won
reputation for truthfulness, reliability, and capacity for scientific
judgment in jeopardy. I can assure my readers
that I do not do this with a light heart.

—C.G. Jung
Flying Saucers: A Modern Myth of Things Seen in the Skies

Behind the lives of ordinary people, extraordinary events often take place. Being alive on earth also means we will die, which seems like a fundamentally bad outcome. One way we cope with the inherent stress provoked by this fatal fact is by telling each other stories of an afterlife. But this one is not my story—it's Galen's, as told by him from his afterlife following his untimely death at age sixteen.

Galen's passing left me shocked and puzzled. His end came quickly and cleanly when a train hit his car at an unguarded railroad crossing, pushing it 1,700 feet. I was told he looked untouched except for a broken leg and broken neck. I couldn't comprehend how his body had been left so blessedly intact, but thankfully I didn't have to ponder more mayhem about his final moments than necessary.

I didn't find out about the accident for several hours, when I received a phone call from the state police on my way to a charity banquet with my mother. Like it was yesterday, I still remember the officer's words, "He didn't make it," before I went into shock. For a nanosecond they did not ring true to me—so certain was I that my son was still alive.

Because the statistical odds of losing a child in a car accident are 1 in 20,000, and in a train collision far lower, it seemed impossible that this would happen to *my* son. I believed such things happened to strangers whose pictures appeared on the evening news.

I recalled the words spoken to me by a mystic soon after Galen was born, implying he would survive into adulthood: "Your son will pick up where your teaching leaves off. Your son will end up counseling you." At the time, I took this unsolicited prophecy as reassurance that my son would follow in his father's footsteps and one day be so wise that I would go to him for advice.

At first his passing seemed a clear refutation of this prediction. Then, as I was able to communicate with him, he in effect became a teacher of events and conditions on the other side by imparting his experience as he perceived it.

I am Galen's father and will be Galen's father for as long as I am a conscious being, regardless of what state or dimension we find ourselves in, as the bond I have with my son transcends time and space. Like many, becoming a parent affected me profoundly. When Galen was seven years old and his mother and I divorced, my hope was that it would be in everyone's best interest, and I turned my life upside down to be there for Galen and to provide everything he needed. Now, even though I am a father whose son has died, at least I know where my son is, and although I will never see him again with my earthly eyes, he is not lost. There are many parents who have children they cannot find, cannot reach, or with whom they cannot communicate either because of abduction or tragic medical conditions.

It is often said that the death of a child is a parent's worst nightmare, but I have found this is not completely true. It is the worst possible nightmare anyone can experience in the earthly sense, without exception. When it became my nightmare, I knew I would not be able to physically survive it, that my heart would not be able to withstand the intensity of my emotions. But then the trauma of Galen's death became a catalyst for profound physical and spiritual transformations. Interventions from unexpected sources eventually led to my being able to compile this book. While the pages that follow contain information that will change both my credibility and reputation as a physician, I have always stood in my truth when it came to what I saw as the ethos of my profession, and I will not waver from that in helping Galen bring forth this book.[1]

My emotional connection with my son has taken me down some unexpected avenues that led to communicating with him after his death and gaining insight into the nature of the other side. At every turn, my bond with Galen grew stronger. Granted, what I have done here with my son is unusual; however, countless parents whose children have passed to the other side would have done no less if the opportunity presented itself. I was prepared for the effort involved in connecting with Galen after he had passed, due to my experiences studying and working with trance mediums in the early 1970s as a volunteer in the now long-disbanded parapsychology lab at the UCLA Neuropsychiatric Institute. Then in January 2007, a year before Galen's death, I came across the first article outside of journals dealing with psychic research

---

[1] For instance, I have been very outspoken about the role of environmental factors in the current "autism" epidemic (KP Stoller, "Les Incompetents: My Open Letter to the American Academy of Pediatrics," *Medical Veritas* 5 [2008]: 1699–1700 and KP Stoller, "Autism as a Minamata Disease Variant: Analysis of a Pernicious Legacy," *Medical Veritas* 3 [2006]: 772–780, both of which are downloadable at www.pdfdatabase.com).

that seriously regarded communication with the dead through a medium. The study claims to prove certain individuals have a gift that allows them to communicate with a source of information providing accurate details about the deceased.[2] The researchers admit that alternative explanations cannot be excluded, such as something called super-ESP or super-PSI, which is another name for telepathy. We do not know how these communications work, nor do we have a framework for understanding them with the logical mind, despite today's scientific understanding of quantum field theory, or the holographic universe.

Within days of Galen's death, I was communicating with Suzy Ward and Terri Daniel,[3] mothers in contact with their sons who had passed. They told me that not only was communication with Galen possible but Galen had the same agreement with me that their sons had with them—to bring forward clear communication from their dimension. This new goal propelled me forward to do the very difficult inner work necessary to build a bridge to my son.

My Life after Life originated through the assistance of helpers both seen and unseen. I began journaling about two weeks after Galen passed, when it became clear that he was trying to communicate with me. If I was becoming delusional, I thought it best to keep a good record of it. By day I was a physician coping with the demands of my work, but at night I would write for several hours, documenting events unfolding in my inner life.

After two years of journaling hundreds of pages about my experiences in what I called my "training sessions," I produced a

[2] J. Beischel and G.E. Schwartz, "Anomalous Information Reception by Research Mediums Demonstrated Using a Novel Triple Blind Protocol," *Explore* 3, no. 1 (2007): 23–27.

[3] Terri Daniel is the author of *A Swan in Heaven: Conversations Between Two Worlds* and *Embracing Death: A New Look at Grief, Gratitude and God*. See http://www.SwanInHeaven.com.

voluminous tome no one will ever read. Then, after the second anniversary of his passing, Galen asked me how the book was coming along. I responded by saying that my ponderous journal would need a lot of work if it were ever to become a book anyone would read. Galen said he was not interested in my book, explaining, "That is *your* story." Galen was interested in telling his own story, and he wanted me to write it down for him.

Ever since, I have been as attentive as an old-time archivist dutifully hand recording the recollections of a witness to a piece of history that would otherwise have been lost. I have made every effort to keep the language as true as possible to the intention behind Galen's words as I perceived them. Galen reviewed each chapter, and if he wanted something modified, it was. Anything I wanted to say was put it in editor's notes, which end each chapter.

Galen wanted to describe his post-earth experience free of the distortions and embellishments that often filter in when humans pen communications from a higher dimensional station. There is no way of measuring how well he did in that arena, so readers are free to take or leave anything that does not resonate with them.

Our perception creates what we see as our reality, and we all have slightly different perceptions, if for no other reason than we all perceive from a slightly different vantage point. We assume a lot about everyone and everything around us, but many of these assumptions are illusions. Although there is general conformity in the environment at the third dimension level, Galen indicated, outside of this dimension perceptions alter quickly.

First and foremost Galen, during his earth life, considered himself a truth seeker, and still does. Therefore, I have done my best to keep the narrative true to his experience as it was conveyed to me. Even though what he describes is fantastical, fantasy was not an intentional part of this story, although it could be construed as just *my* fantasy. But if it is not fantasy, as I believe, then it is a landmark record of a journey shared by a being who wants us to know something important that will enhance our experience in our current dimension.

It is likely that if Galen had remained on earth, he would have become a teacher after many more years of education and experience. Due to the accelerated learning in his dimension, he is fulfilling part of that mission as an author, even though he will only be nineteen years old in earth time when this book is first published.

A lot of deference is generally given to a grieving parent, so much so that if I had written a novel about what I fantasized my son might be doing in some imaginary reality, it might be viewed as pathetic but would at least fall under acceptable norms and be politely tolerated without causing significant repercussions. However, suggesting that this is something other than a fictional work crosses many boundaries. While entertaining the possible existence of a continuum principle, which allows sentient beings to survive the death of their physical bodies, is fine for private speculation or in the context of family beliefs, it is not typically acceptable in other areas of our lives. As the saying goes, there is nothing wrong with talking to the dead, but there is a real problem when you think you are getting an answer back. I therefore ask readers to suspend their disbelief enough to consider that somehow bridges were built between our world and another to allow this book to be written.

At my son's memorial service, his algebra teacher spoke about Galen's effort to convince him that math wasn't real. At first I thought how typical it was for Galen to make a philosophical argument to get out of doing his math work. After all, if math is just a mental construct with no basis in reality, then why bother learning all its complex structures and formulas? Pondering the same dilemma thirty years ago concerning medical school, I'd asked my mentor, "If disease is an illusion, then why bother learning about it in such detail?" My mentor said that while I was correct in understanding disease as an illusion, it was very real to those who had it. Similarly, the events recounted in this narrative were real for me—all too real.

Actually, my concern is not so much about reader disbelief as it is about those with poor problem-solving skills who do believe it and think suicide is a viable option for seeking a fresh start elsewhere. Regarding this misperception, Galen makes it clear that suicide provides a fresh start involving years spent in an unpleasant limbo.

Ultimately what matters is not whether readers believe in the veracity of this book's contents or consider my son a fictional protagonist, but whether the story itself facilitates a broader understanding of universal laws and truths. The descriptions my son provides stand on their own, even if taken as complete fabrication, for in the end the heart recognizes wisdom, whether it arises from a fairy tale or an encyclopedia.

It is Galen's intention that this book be the first of many in an anthology he calls the Death Walker series. Recognizing this series as both a chronicle of my son's present existence and a repository of ancient wisdom, I intend to do everything possible to make it a reality.

Prologue
(The Strangest Dream I Ever Had)

As the winds turned too gusty for paintball, I headed for the interstate to return to my mom's house, about forty-five minutes away.
My iPod provided suitable background music as I headed home,
but I had the sense that things were out of sync in my world.
Maybe I had stayed up too late the night before or hadn't been
eating well. Whatever it was, something didn't feel right.

I was taking my familiar route on I-25, which, when it reaches
Santa Fe, curves southeast for a while as it follows the southern
end of the Sangre de Cristo Mountains. From there I planned to
take an exit just past Pecos, double back on a side road, cross
some railroad tracks, and arrive home.

For a couple of moments while driving this familiar stretch of
highway, I thought my senses were playing tricks on me as if I had
taken off the special glasses they give you at a 3-D movie. I was not
seeing double, but my vision, while vivid, was out of sync. The hum
of the engine, the whistle of the wind, and the rumble of tires all
seemed disconnected as well, appearing to come from somewhere
other than where such sounds originate.

I was glad when I finally saw my exit, but then my iPod started
acting up, moving the percussion track two beats behind the rest of
the music. As I rolled to a stop at the railroad tracks, I decided it might
be wind gusts creating too many positive ions in the air that was acti-
vating my weird sensations. Closing my eyes for a moment, I saw
dancing lights and heard unfamiliar sounds. I felt my body moving,
but I also felt protected. Then suddenly I heard the sound of metal,

followed by a tremendous silence and utter darkness. Eventually the lights and sounds returned, yet none seemed real. I could hear my name spoken every so often, but what was being said and by whom didn't seem to matter. In between the voices, I could hear a faint ringing that started to transform them into a crystalline tone. And then I heard a very clear bell tone in the distance, like the sound a crystal goblet makes when you run your finger around the rim of the glass.

I looked in the direction of the bell and saw what appeared to be another version of myself standing beside me. But this other self was much taller than I am, easily over seven feet, and had a luminescent quality.

He said, "What is it that you want to do?"

This other self beamed a quality that seemed to contain the essence of everyone I had ever loved in my life, so I knew I wanted to follow this version of myself toward the sound of the bell. But he seemed to know my answer without my having to say the words, and he placed a little silver cup in my right hand, pressing it into my palm and folding my fingers over it. At that moment, the bell tone became louder and the other sounds faded away. When the clear ringing sound was all I could hear, I moved peacefully forward with myself, hand in hand.

As we walked along a path, I became more aware of my environs. The landscape was familiar—rolling hills dotted with small pine and juniper trees and scrubby sage, with mountains in the distance. But something was different. It was like looking through a View-Master toy, which lets you observe stereo-slides using a plastic binocular device that produces backlit 3-D images. There was a backlit quality to the light around me, and the plants and trees projected little luminescent accents, as if fine fiber-optic filaments inside them were transmitting light.

The fact that I wasn't waking up from this apparent dream made me want to figure out what this place was about. But the more my mind came up with explanations, the more unfocused my environment became, which was disconcerting. Without wanting to appear too conspicuous, I gazed at this other version of myself, trying to understand how the fact that I had a twin brother had been kept from me all this time. I wanted to touch one of the nearby plants to see how real it was, but I did not want to let go of the hand I was holding.

CHAPTER 1

The Chairs

Still walking hand in hand with my twin, I came to a grassy meadow in which two chairs faced each other, beckoning us to sit down. My twin brought his left hand over to my right hand, which was still clutching the small silver cup, gently encouraging my hand to open while he held the little cup in front of me as if presenting me with a trophy. He then handed me the cup, and as he did I noticed how large his fingers were. He asked, "Do you remember today?"

Now, that is an unusual question to be asked in a dream, I thought to myself. *Did I remember today?* I remembered waking up that Saturday morning, December 1, at the house of a friend from my teen theater group in Santa Fe, New Mexico. I had been rehearsing for the double role of Fagan and Bill Sikes for next month's production of *Oliver!* After two years, I had earned the privilege of not only playing the lead but taking on a second major character as well. My friend and I were planning to get together again later that day, weather permitting, to play paintball, but first I had to meet my grandmother for lunch.

My grandmother had come out from Los Angeles every Thanksgiving for the last ten years—ever since we had moved there from Southern California—and visited for a couple of weeks. She would stay at my dad's house, where I lived every other week since my parents' divorce ten years ago. Normally, I would split my time between my mom's place in Rowe, a small community near Pecos, and my dad's house in Santa Fe, but I'd spend extra time there when Grandma was visiting. This year was different, however. I had moved from my dad's house in June, after he had invited his girlfriend and her five-year-old daughter to move in with us. That scene was definitely not for me. I was so angry with him for doing it that I refused to speak with him, even though he texted me every few days.

My plan on December 1 was to meet Grandma at the Zia Diner at half past noon, near the heart of this adobe city 7,000 feet above sea level. But as I drove to the diner something wasn't exactly right, although I couldn't put my finger on it. The car—my mom's white Honda station wagon—seemed to be running okay, so I shook off the feeling and parked behind the restaurant.

Grandma was already at the diner when I arrived. We hugged, and I realized I now towered over this gentle, caring woman I'd looked up to all my life. I was hungry, having skipped breakfast, as usual, so I ordered a cheese pizza without sauce and a Sprite.

While waiting for our lunch to arrive, Grandma gave me a bag of gifts she had brought, since she didn't know if she would see me later in the month. I pulled them out of the bag one by one, but first I opened an envelope with her card, and to my delight it contained $200, which I said I would use to buy a jacket. There was also a gift from my dad, a cool-looking translucent orange water bottle filled with all kinds of safety knickknacks for the car, an LED flashlight, and a frame he had made of the watercolor *Okami Lone Wolf* that I had placed on his office computer some time ago as desktop wallpaper.

Then Grandma asked me to reconcile with my dad, who was waiting at a nearby shopping center in case I would do so today.

Hearing that, I stood up, without finishing my pizza, and said I needed to help a musician move a piano, though the piano ordeal was actually a scheduled paintball fight; I wanted my grandma to think I was doing something worthwhile. I told her to give the pizza to my dad's dog, Sprout, who was a real pizza hound, but she insisted I take it with me.

As we left the restaurant, she asked me something she had never asked me before—to kiss me on the cheek—so I bent down and received my kiss.

I paused for a moment, looking up at my twin. I could not remember anything past being kissed by my grandmother, and was perplexed by the loss of memory.

"That is all right," my twin said, "but each time you do remember something, hold this cup out in front of you and it will help you remember and understand where you are."

As I had been recalling events, the silver cup had been vibrating in my palm and seemed to gradually get heavier.[1] I summoned my courage and asked him, "Where am I?"

"Your earth body has passed away, and you are in a different dimension. It takes time for the mind to let go of what is so familiar," he said matter-of-factly.

"Is this heaven?"

"It is if you want it to be," he answered.

I was not overjoyed upon hearing this bit of news. I immediately started to worry that it would affect my parents and my grandmother.

I sat on the chair for a while, not knowing what to do or think next. I kept getting confused trying to figure out how I could be in heaven, because I certainly did not feel dead. Out of the corner

---

[1] On entering the earth dimension as a newborn, I later learned, each individual is given a silver cord, and from that cord the silver cup is made, which contains all the experiences of that individual.

of my eye, the chair across from me looked empty, but when I looked at it straight on my twin was sitting there.

I drifted in and out of this surreal space, doing my best to adjust my perceptions, like turning a radio knob to get the sweet spot of the signal and minimize the static. There was nature all around me, but if I took my focus off of it there was nothing around me. When I engaged myself emotionally in the present moment, I could see what was in front of me. If I returned my focus to my mind, there was nothing in front of me, the air around me didn't move, and nothing felt alive. Then as I became present again with my surroundings, they would reappear. This was completely different from earth, where one's environment is always so present you want to shut it out at times. Here I was a link in the chain of my own perceptions! If I wanted to participate with my environment, I had to expand my emotional connection with it.

I wanted very much to be back on earth, especially with my father, and definitely did not want to be in this place. But as it turned out, this anguish was the only bit of suffering I experienced, and it was gone an instant later.

"If you have a question, hold up your cup in front of you," my companion said.

I held my cup up and asked, "Why do I feel so weak?"

"You are not yet connecting to the wholeness that is around you," he answered.

I already seemed to know what that meant, because I'd already discovered the nuance of projecting myself outward and connecting to what was in front of me. If I did this well enough, I would not just visually perceive but would also be nurtured. It felt good to connect, and I needed to just follow the feeling without over-thinking the process.

"So, I am dead then," I said, not really asking a question.

With a wry smile, he retorted, "How can you be dead if you are talking to me?"

"You know, *dead!*" I said, realizing almost all my questions were being answered with more questions and while there was something familiar and almost reassuring about that it was also very frustrating. "Of course, you are going to tell me I am not dead, just existing in a different dimension," I said.

"It is true the body you knew is no longer. You can define yourself as dead if you insist, but you are really never dead," he replied.

"Okay, then, if this is heaven, where are all the dogs?" Dogs were always a big part of my life on earth, and I was in my second year of learning to train assistance dogs for people with disabilities, so I assumed heaven for me would be a place with dogs.

Suddenly I could hear dogs barking, and as if the doors on a thousand kennels had swung open, the meadow in which we were sitting was now full of dogs panting, barking, and wagging their tails.

I laughed with joy, but my laughter reminded me that I'd been very happy with my life on earth and would have been content to continue on with it. Not understanding why I had died, I asked, "How did this happen?"

My companion then told me about the train hitting me.

I was unaware that time is completely different in the dimension in which I'd found myself and that things take place here when they are supposed to, not in keeping with any clock or calendar. So I had no way of knowing that only six hours had passed on earth since the accident until my twin said, "Your father has an awareness of where you are and he is asking you if you are okay."

"I am absolutely okay, and I miss you," I said, directing this statement to my dad, although I felt a little exasperated at having my attention directed back to events taking place on earth.

"He wants to know what you are doing," my twin said.

Actually, I didn't engage in most of this conversation until months later, by my time. Time here is more spiral than linear, and I wasn't allowed to fully participate in this conversation until

I was ready. Universal time, as opposed to linear time of the third dimension, has an emotional factor, so things take place when it is most suitable for them to take place.

"He always wanted the best for you, and if this is in your best interest then he is just going to deal with it," my twin continued.

I had total awareness of my father's pain and the intense emotions others were feeling. But I was also protected from the desperate grief that was being generated, which ranged from sorrow to borderline insanity.

"Don't be mad at my mom," I said. This was a request my dad did not understand at the time.

"Your father is asking, 'What are we to do now?'" my twin reported.

"There is nothing you need to do for me on earth," I replied, without understanding the full implication of his question.

Turning my attention to my other self, I asked, "You are my identical twin brother, aren't you?"

"There is no way I am your twin brother because I look so much better than you do!"

I shot him a look befitting a smart aleck, and he said, "I am an aspect of yourself and the soul family of which you are a part. I stood with you before you drew your first breath on earth, as I am with you now to teach you how to thrive here. I am your teacher and your father's teacher."

My first lesson, if you will, was that there was no separation between my environment and myself. By projecting, I could stimulate the environment around me to show me where I was. Then I learned what it meant to listen in this dimension. Listening wasn't only about hearing words that were spoken; it was also about being aware of the many layers of intent and the emotions behind it.

Next, I learned to trust and love because I couldn't engage my environment unless I projected trust and love. Although interaction with the environment occurs differently on earth, you also cannot truly be a human until you learn to love.

It seemed like forever before I was fully prepared to engage my new surroundings. At that point, my teacher asked me to stand and handed me a beautiful silver chain, which attached to the cup. I placed it around my neck, and the small cup hung near my heart.

❧ ❧ ❧

Editor's note: The night of Galen's passing, I had left Santa Fe with my mother to attend a charity dinner in Albuquerque. In the early evening, more than three hours after the event, I received the call about the accident from the state police while approaching the first Albuquerque exit off the interstate. The first person I phoned was the actor Adam Baldwin as he, his wife Ami, and their children had been close with Galen and myself for several years. Ami literally talked me back to Santa Fe as my mother and I were in a state of shock.

Several years earlier, I had worked closely with a trance medium capable of connecting to the other side,[2] and it was through her that I made the connection with Galen the night of his accident. It would take me over two years to understand that

---

[2] A decade earlier, I had spent nine months interviewing the guides who came through trance medium Audrey Wrinkles and had great confidence in the accuracy of the information. Their insight into medical matters far exceeded anything I had previously encountered. But not until 1999, when my father died, did I discover her guides could work with problems some have in crossing over. From what my mother had reported to me, my father was stuck haunting their house. Audrey's guides walked me through a visualization—for lack of a better term—during which I approached this confused aspect of my father's persona and made it possible for him to see those who could help him cross.

this moving—and at the time, very confusing—conversation with my son, took place for him at multiple points in universal time, since for me it was taking place all at once in his room, a place he had not seen in six months. Alone in his room, I sobbed, pressing the phone hard to my ear while talking to a woman in a trance whose body was being used by her interdimensional guides to connect with my son, whom I would never see again and who was talking more in riddles to me than not. I didn't understand why this needed to happen, though I also knew there are no accidents and I was going to have to support this transition. That's what I was thinking; what I was feeling was my world was ending and my very existence no longer had purpose.

When the conversation ended, I silently vowed to either talk to Galen myself in his dimension or to die trying. For the first time in my life, I swallowed a strong sedative, and as I was lying in bed it began to kick in. Only vaguely aware that Galen's phone was probably in some plastic bag or on the floor of the destroyed car, I picked up my mobile phone and sent him one last text message: "I love you, Galen."

CHAPTER 2

Matthew's Message

Although I was uncertain what to do next or where to go, I was glad to know I at least had a teacher who appeared as my larger identical twin and a sense that I belonged to everything around me. I soon found I was also able to call dogs to me, which delighted me since dogs had been one of my favorite joys on earth. But they were all imaginary except for one real dog I adopted, or who adopted me. On earth he had been a black lab with a white tuft of hair on his chest. He told me his name was Andrew. He had been a search and rescue dog on earth, so he was skilled at creating joy for humans who were suffering and at recognizing the dead and the subtle energies still hanging around a body. I soon learned that Andy had lost his earth life while looking for survivors in a collapsed building; upon locating someone trapped below him in the rubble, he slipped and fell into the destroyed structure, which caved in around him. At first I just called him "Dog," but he insisted I call him by his given name, so I called him "Andy" for short.

Andy reminded me a little bit of the last dog I had helped train for Assistance Dogs of the West, a black lab named Doc. I had sensed that a disabled Iraqi vet was going to get Doc, so I trained him to salute on command, which came in handy when indeed he was given to a disabled Iraqi vet. Unlike Doc, Andy let me practice projecting my imagination on him so I could change his appearance to match the dogs I had known in the past. It was comforting to be near dogs like those I had been close to on earth.

Later, I found out that the level of consciousness you initially experience here has to do with the maturity level of your soul plus or minus the experience and beliefs of your personality, and that there are many levels both below and above my dimensional station. Andy's consciousness seemed to be as developed as a dog's could get, and was on a par with my own. Actually, everything seemed to be at the same level of experience until I had acclimated enough to deal with the complexity of the other levels. It kept things simple for me, much like a young child having big crayons to color with because they're easier to hold.

Eventually, I left the grassy meadow and, with Andy at my side, began to walk all around this world. At first I ambled through landscapes familiar to me and with which I could comfortably interact, such as high desert terrains and grassy plains. I spent a lot of time walking through Bandelier National Monument as I remembered it, with its many ancestral Pueblo dwellings where families once lived, reminding me of my longing to reconnect with my family. Whenever I reflected on memories of my experiences on earth, my cup would vibrate. If I wanted to ask my teacher a question, I could focus in front of me and he would be there. He still appeared as my larger twin self, because it is easy to see yourself in this dimension, and I was still exploring the easy level—Heaven 101—where things were kept simple for me.

After I had adjusted a little to this dimensional station, I was curious about the events that had taken place during my time crossing over, and I asked my teacher, "I have read stories of what takes place when one crosses over. What happened to the tunnel of light, and why was I not greeted by my adoring relatives?"

"That experience is a truth on some levels of awareness, and is often an implanted memory in those who have near-death experiences. The sum total that happens in that instant is given a form so the mind can recall a memory of beauty, light, and love," my teacher said.

Day became night, and night became day. I felt the warmth of the sun and spent hours pondering under a canopy of brilliant stars. At night I closed my eyes but did not fall asleep or dream in a true sense, as one does on earth when the conscious mind drifts away like a low tide going out to sea and the subconscious mind flows in. Instead, I remained fully conscious all the time, and every so often I would open my eyes to see if Andy was sleeping next to me, which he was. I needed to know he was there, to feel the warmth of his body, to touch his fur and feel him breathing. He loved to play our game of morphing into other dog forms, so sometimes I found him in the shape of a beagle rather than a black lab.

I now began to experiment with transforming my environment through interaction, as I had done with Andy. I created a *Star Wars*–like scene to move through, as well as a Dr. Seuss-like environment. It was like doing CGI without the computer, with everything just coming from my imagination.

While in repose I began to focus on what I wanted to do in this new dimension. My first desire was to understand universal laws and truths, which had far more importance than I thought such things had on earth. In a way, I wanted to follow a path to higher learning, but I also wanted to be able to communicate directly with my father.

It had been ten days in linear earth time since I had passed—something I learned later—and I was alone with Andy, walking along a deserted beach with ocean waves crashing against the sand, creating a salty spray. In all my travels up to that point, I had never seen a city, a car, or a single soul except Andy, so I was surprised when I looked far down the beach and saw a male figure walking toward me. I had never seen my teacher appear to me from such a distance; instead he'd show up by my side when I called him. And this man was not coming from my imagination, since his gait indicated someone with a clear intention outside my control.

Soon a blond young man with a kind face stood before me, a slight shimmer of light around his body—which I later learned occurred with subtle dimensional shifts—much like some of the scenery I first encountered while walking toward the chairs. He introduced himself as Matthew, but I said, "I don't think I know who you are."

"I know who you are," Matthew replied.

The sound of the waves crashing on the beach silenced, and the whole environment seemed to hold its breath. I quickly called in my teacher to explain who this was.

"This is Matthew Ward, who comes to you through a connection between your father and his mother, as she moved through the same healing process your father must now move through. She has already developed the ability to communicate with her son," my teacher said. "There is a need and a request."

"Oh, *that* Matthew!" I exclaimed, recalling a boy, now a young man, who had lost his life in a car accident in 1980, when he was seventeen—not much older than I was. My father would often bore me with what I considered dubious messages from Matthew that his mother would post monthly online.[1] He looked so much more mature than in the little photo on his mother's Web site.

Matthew said, "Welcome to nirvana. I am here as a messenger to your father. Is there anything you wish to say to him?"

Excited about the chance to send a message to my father, even if through an intermediary, I quickly spoke about the possibility for future communication and collaboration between us, encouraged by the example set by Matthew and his mother, something I now understood and valued more than during my life on earth, as its potential was now much clearer.

---

[1] http://matthewbooks.com/mattsmessage.htm.

My exchange with Matthew was all too brief. At one point, I looked down at my feet because the leading edge of a wave swept by my ankles, and when I looked back Matthew was no longer there. My teacher said prayers and desires from earth had allowed me to meet Matthew to assist my father. He also said that I would not have normally been introduced to someone so adept at moving in and out of dimensions at that point in my orientation.

My father received the message that Matthew gave his mother with only the slightest interpretation. The message gave him some relief for his pain in that moment as the words went right to his heart:

Dear soul Ken,

This is Matthew lovingly greeting you. I asked my mother to let me assure you that, in time, you and Galen will be able to communicate the same as she and I. Please do not expect to talk directly with him immediately; your tender condition is rampant with urgent emotions that must be felt and transmuted before he can reach you for a lengthy conversation.

So I am here in his stead to tell you your son is strong and vibrant, quickly adjusting to the realm of nirvana, and greeting souls of many lifetimes. He asks me to tell you also how proud he is of you, the soul he now knows as well as your aspect as his father, and how thrilled he is to return in spirit so he can proceed with your collaborative mission free of earth's heavy encumbrances. He is transmitting loving energy to you and is joined by myriad other highly evolved light beings to ease your passage through grief. Let Galen's message to you reach your heart, knowing that he is with you more purely than in the physical.

I add that each time you smile or laugh, and also weep, which you must, Galen is doing the same, and the love bond eternally shared that is healing for you is at the same time propelling your beloved son forward in his service.

After my meeting with Matthew, I asked my teacher, "How is it that Matthew can send a message to my father but I can't?"

"There are steps and levels you need to move through. You are in a type of training where you can mature your form so it is better integrated with the frequency in which you now find yourself, and then you will have greater movement. Matthew is on a level where he is more integrated." I wasn't pleased to hear that I had steps and levels to move through, for on earth I took pride in being at the head of the class, at least in the classes I cared about.

I made several vain attempts to call Matthew back. I almost hurt my head trying to will that into place. It was then I began to understand that while there is will there is also timing and allowance. The message from Matthew to my father may have been given to him out of grace, but it dangled a carrot in front of me—I wanted to move in and out of dimensions, deliver messages back, and rescue others. I had been happy with my nature walks and the presence of Andy until Matthew showed up and made me realize there were possibilities of which I had not been aware. But this was not something I could change through sheer will alone. Still, I had a sort of tantrum anyway – you have no idea how far a rock can go in heaven when you throw it in frustration.

My teacher explained the kind of transformation that was necessary before I might have such an ability, saying, "There is truth as well as illusion to this dimension, just as there is on earth. And while there is a place that the mind perceives as real, when you mature, the mind leaves behind the illusion." My illusion was that I could do exactly what Matthew could do and do it immediately, but I was not aligning with my now or allowing for synchronization. I wasn't letting the moment teach me, for the will is a tool to *move* energy but not *create* energy. And so I learned the difference between will and manifestation.

I could imagine almost anything I wanted within the confines of the world I now inhabited, but I longed for something else, though it was not clear to me what that was. Still, once my intention to communicate with my father was clear, my teacher told me how music and art could allow me access to my father's dreamtime. He said that music, art, and literature have very high soul energy. Because my dad had a special interest in them and was thus aligned with their energy, I could attempt to access his subconscious mind through them. He commented further that on earth there is an under-appreciation of the role of music, art, and literature as links to the higher dimensions. The tones, colors, and qualities of music, art, and literature are utilized by those who reside in the higher dimensions; therefore, it is through art, music, and literature that higher consciousness can be accessed. It was use of this knowledge that first allowed me to let my dad know I was here and thus end my sense of isolation.

With the instructions my teacher gave me, I returned to the grassy meadow with the chairs, closed my eyes, and focused in front of me, creating the image of my father. In this way I gained access to the files of his subconscious mind and then pondered how best to send a message to him using information stored in them. It was like going through a card shop and picking out a card with the message I wanted to send. There were living memory images like the living paintings Harry Potter saw on the wall of Hogwarts Castle, as well as hundreds of songs. In this space I could become the actor because my father was, in a sense, an actor, and I could become the music because my father was the music.

To make it very clear to him where the dream I intended to send was coming from, I first selected a set of fond memories my father had of me and strung them together into a short montage, then for the musical accompaniment I went to the section on Broadway plays and found a song under *Camelot* with lyrics that were exactly what I wanted for this dream. *Camelot* was easy to access because my father's energy resonated with it. In my father's memory the song I picked was associated with love and bittersweet emotions, as it was about a king with a tender heart that was broken by a woman who desired something else. It opened with the well-known lines:

> If ever I would leave you
> It wouldn't be in summer.[2]

Since the information in this dream was already in my father's mind, all I had to do was use my intention to activate the memories in a certain sequence when I sensed he was open. When the dream was delivered, my father woke up immediately and knew I had sent it.

☙ ☙ ☙

Editor's note: On December 11, the eve of my visit to a clinic in Sacramento, California, where I was treating brain-injured adults and children utilizing hyperbaric oxygen, Matthew's mother delivered his message. She told me that I had an agreement with Galen to communicate between dimensions similar to her agreement with her son. My emotional response to hearing the message was equivalent to that of a drowning man locking his grip around a tethered life preserver. The next day in Sacramento, I received the *Camelot* dream and woke immediately. I was at first distraught from the array of images triggering fond memories that had been strung together like a slide show, along with the tune from *Camelot* that stuck in my mind.

It took a couple of hours to fully sink in that this montage had been created as a message from Galen, who had loved Broadway musicals more than anything besides dogs, and whose dream was to have a career in theater. One might assume (incorrectly), that

---

Alan Jay Lerner and Frederick Loewe.

these first attempts at communication between Galen and myself would have greatly modulated the level of grief and despair I was experiencing. In a sense they did modulate my emotions, paradoxically intensifying them as if I were being pushed to process at a quicker pace. I felt so emotionally beat up about six months after Galen passed that I actually asked him to stop sending me songs unless I was first invited to receive one.

I needed the communication between us to be in a different form because I felt the intense emotions I had to deal with after hearing some of these songs had become counterproductive. The tune that finally did me in was "Turn Around," sung by a woman's voice so beautiful it could have come from heaven, and it probably did. She began:

Where are you going, my little one, little one...[3]

There I was, lying in bed in the still of the night and hearing a woman's voice, lovely and warm, singing this bittersweet song in perfect pitch. The experience taking place in my conscious awareness was so intimate, it almost felt like a violation. To be lying in bed in the middle of the night emotionally raw, hearing without warning such a tearful song in heavenly fidelity, was difficult to bear. Consequently, "Turn Around" was the last song I ever received.

---

[3] Harry Belafonte, Malvina Reynolds, and Alan Greene.

CHAPTER 3

"The Great I"

Creating a dreamtime conversation with my father gave me the same sense of accomplishment one gets from a hole in one or from wiggling one's big toe after being paralyzed. Looking back on this now, wiggling the big toe was about all I did accomplish, but in that moment it meant everything to me. The song from *Camelot*, the first of many songs I sent to my father, which he came to call "heaven tunes," was essentially the same type of play I did with Andy. I just had to sculpt music for my dad's dreams in such a way that he would know the messages were from me. And while I also attempted to send many such messages to my grandmother and my mother, I never received a response from anyone other than my father, helping me appreciate how grief and fear form barriers to communication from my dimension to those I love on earth. I learned how grief dulls intuition and, if it merged with fear, flips it into superstition. Grief and ensuing depression were the only feelings many people from my earth life were experiencing, as if all the colors had been taken out of their sunsets. Finding it regrettable to witness, I directed my efforts at communication mostly to my father, who seemed best able to receive it.

And just as there were barriers to communication between dimensions, so were there portals where information could be exchanged with greater ease. It was part of my training to work with these variations in communication potential.

I was also able to communicate with my father through my teacher. By some grace or allowance that I did not question, my teacher would tell me what my father was trying to communicate to me, and I, in turn, would give my teacher a reply as if writing my father a letter from summer camp. I also had conversations with my teacher concerning observations I had about the nature of the dimension I was in, to verify and help explain my perceptions. Sometimes my teacher would just nod or provide a brief comment; other times he would tease, saying, "Well, wasn't that obvious?" The ribbing was a constant in our conversations, which is exactly how I had talked to my friends and even my father, making it comfortingly familiar banter.

I understood completely that what I saw from day to day was essentially my creation, and yet the material from which these beautiful landscapes were composed was also connected to the dimension in which I existed. I knew that this was no holodeck from *Star Trek: The Next Generation*. My understanding was evolving beyond elementary experiences, and my awareness of the dynamics of this place was expanding.

I asked my teacher, "I understand that here the sun rises, the moon comes up, and the stars shine due to the expectations I have from my earth experience. But earth is a planet, part of a system that revolves around a star. This place is not a planet, so what is it that holds you and me, anyone or anything, together in this dimension?"

I passed my arm through Andy's body as if he weren't there (I had asked Andy for permission to do this demonstration in advance), making the point that whatever laws of physics were in force on earth certainly didn't apply here. Then I continued, "I couldn't do this on earth, except in my mind, so am I now just a thought that doesn't physically exist anywhere?"

My teacher answered, "Thoughts are pulses of energy, so on one level you are a thought as just about everything is, but thought energy gathers together and follows a form. That form has an intelligence that creates itself in this space."

I had to ponder his answer for a while because it was very abstract and pushed the limit of what I could comprehend. "Are you talking about molecules?" I asked.

"No, there is something smaller than a molecule, smaller than an atom, smaller than electrons, until the energy becomes infinite, and it is gathered together and supports the rest," my teacher responded.

My silver cup vibrated as I remembered an entry in my school journal I had written just weeks before I left:

> What do you know? As far as my philosophy goes…nothing. Nothing is undeniably true. There is no such thing as an absolute fact.
>
> There are scientific reasons, of course—theories of such particles like gravitons (theoretical elemental particles of no mass [part of string theory] that hold everything together), which by scientific law should not be able to exist yet the universe can't exist without them. Everything that is definite contradicts its own existence by being definite. No matter stays in the same form constantly. Deep down everything is always changing. Nothing is undeniably this or that. Everything that exists also does not. The only undeniable truth is that nothing can be true.

I understood this now to the very core—what was theoretical on earth was reality here.

"No one has traveled to this point—the finite of the infinite—so it is not known how many layers and levels this energy has, but what is known is what comes out from this source and creates itself. Now, I want you to see something." My teacher swept his arm across the sky.

I started to notice a pattern of energy I had never seen before, and yet there was something familiar. The sky was still its perfect color of blue, but as I softened my vision I clearly saw a subtle stream of energy being drawn toward a center point of light as if I were looking directly up into the core of a water spout moving into the sky, but this was not water. Nor was it anything to do with portals and vortexes. Recalling a childhood memory reminiscent of this phenomenon, I asked, "What is that?"

"That is what we call 'The Great I.'"

"Eye?" I asked.

"You can see it as that, but we call it 'The Great I,' as in the letter *I*."

"Is that God I am looking at?"

"You may label it that," my teacher said. "Others label it something else. It does not matter what it is called. But this is the gathering of intelligent form. This dimension is broad enough to allow you to perceive the incredible depth of all this energy that draws up."

I started to feel a physical pull on my skin, as if every part of my being wanted to join in the flow that was moving toward the light at the center of this cylinder. Up to that moment, I had decided that since I was now dead and in heaven this dimension would be the sum total of my future experiences. But I now realized that there were other dimensions I could also access, giving me a new feeling of the potential for expansion.

"So will my time here come to an end?" I asked.

"Yes," my teacher said. "You have a cycle here, as well. When you have learned all you can from this dimension, you will move into 'The Great I' and find yourself in another place after you have made certain choices. It is not yet time for those choices."

I remembered first seeing this phenomenon on earth at age four or five, and asking my father about it. As I recalled the memory, my silver cup vibrated again and became a bit larger—no longer appearing as a small object that could be pressed into the palm of my hand. In the daytime sky on earth "The Great I" looks different than it does here. There it is an ovoid shape that looks like a giant flower with a smooth but irregular circumference and that changes from sky blue to a translucent violet or indigo. The circumference is constantly undulating as petal-like shapes quickly move toward the center, appearing to fall into a drain while new petals replace those that have disappeared.

When I asked my father what I was seeing in the sky, he knew exactly what I was talking about, having seen it many times himself. He said that this perpetual energy flux in the sky was a manifestation of prana, a visual representation of the force that energetically sustains life on earth. This physical phenomenon can be perceived by many individuals, although never at night because the human eye is not sufficiently developed to detect its presence except against the daytime sky.

I wondered if untold numbers of children had asked their parents or another adult what they were seeing as they gazed at "The Great I," and how many were stifled for having asked. How easy it is to suppress the curiosity of children and thus break their spirits by not acknowledging universal truths. Fortunately, I had a prebirth agreement with my father never to stifle my creative, intuitive, or emotional energy, and he has remained true to it.

Afterward, I tried many times to find the "The Great I" myself but never could see it. I had to content myself with knowing it was there. The awareness that everything cycles caused me to develop a little nervous energy, thinking I had to be busy since one day I would be going somewhere. My teacher teased me often about my push to get things done, and I soon had to balance that feeling because my frustration was affecting my family back on earth, causing my parents and even my grandmother to quicken the pace of their lives, sensing that time, as they perceived it, was running out.

Part of my family's time acceleration was in response to the fact that I had begun to experience my environment and myself differently. There was more of a twenty-one-year-old feeling about who I was, but I didn't stop there. I morphed myself into a twenty-five-year-old me, and then a twenty-eight-year-old. I also wanted to know what it would feel like to be thirty-two and even seventy-five. It made me happy to know I was not going to be stuck as a sixteen-year-old in the wonderful dimension in which I now found myself.

I wanted to understand all the levels of who I was and would have been had I remained on earth, and I used age-hopping to start that process. It didn't take me long to recognize that there was much more to this dimension than I had realized, and with that understanding I actually started to see more—and then create more. For instance, I was able to create a rather cool-looking apartment for myself, which I redecorated a multitude of times. First it was a Manhattan flat, and then I turned it into a splendid baroque villa. I worked with crystalline material to the point where the apartment started to look like Superman's Fortress of Solitude then suddenly morphed into the bridge of the USS Enterprise (of *Star Trek*). I had a lot of fun with this, and was able to sustain a structure without having to stand in front of it. I had a place to go instead of just going someplace. I could leave my home and when I returned it would be just where I had left it. This was the result of setting an intention and leaving it in place, and maintaining it without getting distracted. On earth this would be analogous to setting an intention to manifest something you wanted to do in your life, knowing it would be possible at the right time but without having to remind yourself about it every day.

It was one of the many changes that took place in my level of awareness for having seen "The Great I." In addition to an enhanced ability to create environments, my lessons became increasingly complex and included the knowledge that "The Great I" is in every dimension for it creates the dimensions.

Editors note: I was not much older than Galen when, upon first seeing this phenomenon in the sky, I asked my mother what it was. Because of how important the experience was for me, I remember exactly where I was when I asked this question—just as I remember exactly where I was when Galen asked me the same question—but for my five-year-old self no answer would be forthcoming. So it meant a lot to me that I was able to tell my son what I knew to the best of my knowledge, even though my understanding was only partial.

While writing down this chapter I made several halfhearted attempts to again see "The Great I," and although I could sense it I could not see it until late one afternoon when I pulled up to my home very groggy after an exhausting day. Despite, or perhaps because of, my hypnagogic state, I could see "The Great I" through the windshield of my car just north of the sun, which would be setting in another hour. It looked the same as the first time I had seen it: a collection of translucent indigo-tinted ovoid forms being pulled quickly into the center of the pattern. Now, thanks to Galen, I had a greatly expanded appreciation of what I was looking at.

While Galen was doing his age-hopping, I journaled that I was getting images of Galen at various ages he would never be on earth. These images intruded so obsessively on my waking hours that I finally decided I had to stop torturing myself. Within days, I was informed that Galen had been exploring what it would have been like had he lived to be these various ages. My heart had been torn open so wide I had been able to pick up on Galen's activity in his dimension.

CHAPTER 4

The Hall of Cups

The photonic pattern I perceived as my body had changed in response to being exposed to the rays of "The Great I," providing me with a grand epiphany in understanding myself, but I also wanted to understand agreements I had with members of my family. I did not want to leave my father focused on the tragedy that my young life had ended so quickly. I regretted that I had broken off communication with him for the last six months of my earth life, which only compounded my remorse over leaving everyone in my family with pain due to my passing. While aware that their experience was one to which my soul had agreed, in the moment I felt responsible.

To get a better perspective on the effect of my passing, my family, and my own situation, I consulted my teacher. "I understand my family regards it as tragic that I left at sixteen, but I feel no different at other ages in which I place myself, so is it really a tragedy to die so young?" I asked my teacher.

"At what age would you have preferred to die?"

It was a question for which I had no immediate answer.

"On earth, linear time influences the degree of tragedy. A child dying at six months of age is considered more tragic than a man dying at seventy-three, because he has lived a full life," my teacher continued. "Yet on earth there is no appreciation of how old any given soul is as it leaves. The true tragedy is an inability to love in the moment."

"Yes, it is a tragedy when something is not respected or loved," I said with sadness, remembering how my heart would break thinking about dogs and other animals that did not have love, and even the earth itself. I began to weep because I could feel exactly what the lack of love created on earth—separation and tragedy. I thought the list of what is not appreciated on earth is probably very long, and based on what I knew of human history an inability to love what is present in the moment had plagued humankind for a very long time.

"The soul comes to earth for a certain type of experience so it can learn and grow," my teacher said. "Every life has a purpose, even if it doesn't last beyond the first spark of conception or the individual ends up being a bum on the street or a squirrel in some tree. It is not the length of time one spends on earth that is important, but the reason for coming to earth."

"Earth is one big classroom?" I asked.

"One of many, and as an aspect of your soul, you enrolled for a specific set of courses and also to help others with their coursework."

"An aspect of my soul? What does that mean?" I asked.

"You are an expression of your soul, just as your soul is an expression of 'The Great I,'" my teacher explained.

"What is the coursework that earth offers?" I asked.

"An infinite number of lessons can be learned on earth, but the short answer is 'Learning from the experience of isolation while making choices that have consequences,'" my teacher answered.

"Isolation from what?"

"You forget who you really are and where you came from when you work with human experience. Earth is unique because of this forgetting. While some individuals, especially children, remember a past life or two, this memory serves more as a reminder of where one has been than where one came from. In forgetting, you believe you are separate from the whole of life. There is a greater sense of belonging in the higher planes, whereas life on earth is an experiment in isolation and in bringing about conscious choice through balance. This results in connection, which is something those on higher planes take for granted. They emerge from the birth process knowing where they came from, unlike those on earth."

"But on earth one can choose not to feel separate, right?" I asked.

"Yes, because there is no separation," my teacher replied. "But human consciousness is deeply invested only in what the mind knows. Humans believe that is what makes one conscious, correct? 'I think, therefore I am.' But as you have already learned here, it is only when your perceptions come from a nonmental place that you truly become conscious."

No way could I get to earth in my old material body, but I was still determined to connect with earth. I was now in a place where there was so much more love to give, and I vowed to somehow move it through the dimensions while reestablishing communication with my father. Since I was an aspect of my soul and understanding the soul would lead me to understand why I came to be Galen, I decided to start my exploration of soul with the soul that is my father.

Aware of my intention to explore this idea, my teacher directed me to a stately building that from the outside reminded me of the US Supreme Court. He said this was the Hall of Cups, often called the akashic records—a great library where the cup of each soul is kept. "You can see who your father is and where he has come from by finding his cup," my teacher said.

I entered the expansive pavilion, which was much larger than it appeared to be from the outside. Row after row, stack after stack of goblets, well beyond the horizon, stood before me. While the interior was well illuminated, the glow came solely from an infinite number of silver goblets perfectly arranged on shelves. Each was about eighteen inches high with a mouth eight inches or so in diameter. From what I could tell, no two were identical, as if each one was a snowflake.

The awe I felt at the sight of the enormous Hall of Cups caused some trepidation about being able to find my father's cup among the countless ones before me. Then a librarian appeared and informed me that the cups were arranged in alphabetical order. "You have got to be kidding," I thought to myself, imagining that the alphabet could hardly handle such a vast collection, but I stepped forward holding my father's first name in my thoughts.[1]

Instantly, countless rows of goblets flew by me in a flash, and before me, on one of the shelves, was my father's cup. I looked closely into the large, ornate cup, which at first was like looking at the vastness of the night sky, except for a slight ripple on the surface, giving the sense of gazing at the cosmos through a pool of water. The experience that followed was not unlike looking into Professor Dumbledore's Pensieve,[2] an object used in *Harry Potter* lore to review memories. By looking inside my father's cup, I was able to see who he had been, where he had come from, and why the two of us had an agreement to be connected in this life. I was also able to see many of the personalities his soul had been in the past and also the archetypes his soul had worked with. A noble warrior wearing a golden breastplate caught my eye right away,

---

[1] At the time, I did not realize I was actually being drawn by a specific tone, but the alphabetical order story made the process comprehensible to me.

[2] A magical stone basin used by the fictional Harry Potter while in his fourth year at Hogwarts School of Witchcraft and Wizardry.

[3] Archetypes are patterns used by the soul to call forward a set of experiences, such as the healer, the hero, the mermaid, the sage-warrior, the victim, and the damsel in distress.

but more importantly I realized that my soul and his had been companions during many lifetimes, and on many occasions he had laid his life down for me. Looking inside my father's cup completely changed the way I thought about my lineage, and I spent a long time trying to understand events that had taken place while I was on earth and their connection with what I saw in the cup—my true genealogy!

As I further explored the Hall of Cups, I learned that the cups are more than vessels of memory involving sojourns on earth. They hold experiences from all the various dimensions the soul has utilized. In addition, the cups hold information about which dimensions are in play at the same time the earth dimension is being utilized, because the soul usually has multiple aspects active at the same moment. Because the cups hold all experiences, it is not necessary to repeat lessons that have been learned. You may still need to understand the experiences, but to do so you don't need to relive them again to the same extent.

In looking at the cups, it became increasingly clear they differed greatly in their degree of ornateness. And I began to feel dejected realizing that the cup hanging around my neck was so small and plain compared to the others.

"What's wrong—do you have cup envy?" my teacher teased. I assumed my cup was just an aspect of my master cup located in the Hall of Cups. It seemed that my cup only held information from my recent life on earth and eventually I would add its contents to my master cup, and in so doing the master cup would become a little larger and more ornate. I mused about my little cup adding a Boy Scout-sized merit badge to the master cup, although I don't think the badge will have anything to do with train avoidance. My teacher informed me, however, that it isn't entirely accurate to say my small cup is only about my one life, as each of these individual life cups are a holographic-like representation of the master cup—that is, the whole spectrum of experience contained in my master cup can be accessed in the small cup, just as the master cup is a holographic-like representation of "The Great I."

"There is only one cup," my teacher said.

For the moment, I was content with not having to drag around a huge goblet, but I did want complete clarity about why and to whom I had been born, and my teacher told me the reason I was interested in clarity about my earth experience as Galen was because I would be taking most of it to my next life when the time came. This revelation intrigued me and led me to search for my own cup in the Hall of Cups. As I held my name in my mind, again untold rows of cups flashed by in an instant until the shelf where my cup was supposed to be was revealed. But there was only a faint dust ring marking the place where a cup had been, indicating someone had moved it. When I asked my teacher to explain this to me, he said, "It is not time for you to view your own master cup, as you are calling it, for this cup is still active for you. When it is time for your transition from this dimension, you will bring your cup here and place it on the shelf, where it will transform into the master cup." That meant the reason I could not see my own master cup was because the little cup hanging from my neck actually was the master cup.

My concern turned again to my father because now, especially after visiting his cup, I could feel his intense despair, and I was very concerned that his body and mind could not withstand his profound grief. To get more perspective, I asked my teacher, "Will my father become ill with his grief and deep sense of tragedy about my leaving at only sixteen?"

He answered, "Your father must choose between two roads. One road will lead to great depression and physical illness, causing his body to give out. The other road will allow him to move forward with his own explorations, which will mirror what you will be working on in this dimension."

I felt a sudden surge of emotion well up and the impulse to get a message to my dad, so he would know there was a way forward and he didn't have to suffer any longer. I wanted to tell him that tragedy is just the lack of love in any situation. I held my cup out in front of me as if it were a megaphone and glanced at my teacher who gave me an encouraging look and indicated what he wanted me to say, even though it seemed a little mean to be saying it. Then with every ounce of emotion I could muster, I yelled, *"What age would you have preferred that I died?"* To make sure he knew this message was from me, I sent a show tune along with it. As my dad knew I was supposed to be reprising the role of Fagin in just a couple of earth weeks, I sent Fagin's big finale song from *Oliver!*, entitled "Reviewing the Situation."

At 5:00 a.m., twenty-seven days after I left the earth dimension, my father heard my message, and it changed everything for him.

෮෧ ෮෧ ෮෧

Editor's note: I was lying in the bed Galen would have been sleeping in at my mother's house in Los Angeles when I received this message. The words were clear and unambiguous, but the voice was neutral, so I would not necessarily have known it was from Galen without the tune from *Oliver!* that accompanied it. This was the third heaven tune he had sent; the second, "Bombs Away," by the Police, had arrived a week before to get my mind off of the song from *Camelot*, which is a bit of a tearjerker because you know how the story will end. "Bombs Away" is just a fun song with an unusual chorus:

> *Bombs away, but we're O.K.*
> *Bombs away, in old Bombay* [4]

---

[4] From Zenyattà Mondatta (A&M); words and music by Stewart Copeland.

The question "What age would you have preferred that I died?" was so unlike anything I could imagine that it further reinforced the fact that I had just had my first explicit verbal conversation with my son, even though it was one way. While my answer to the question would have been "After me," the question caught me off guard in my hypnopompic state, between sleep and wakefulness, so I could do nothing but wake up completely jubilant in the predawn darkness.

I went back to sleep only to experience grief so intense that I woke myself up wailing Galen's name. All the joy I had felt just a couple of hours before was completely gone, and I was in the opposite emotional state, devastated. It took me months to understand that hearing my son communicate with me had shifted my reality so acutely that I immediately began releasing lifetimes of grief at an accelerated rate.

Hearing my son speak to me set me on a path where the unimaginable—having to experience the release of more and more grief—became my everyday reality. The brief moment of joy on hearing his words for the first time was followed by waves of intense emotions that went on for the next eighteen months. I had to process events and memories in my life that normally don't get worked on till one is in one's own afterlife.

I never asked Galen what he saw looking into my cup, because truly I didn't care. I actually have spotty memories of my last two earth incarnations and that is more than enough to have to take in. Knowing about the lives he saw in my cup would have been entertainment for my mind at best, and I was not interested in entertainment. I figured if there was something I was supposed to know I would be told, but I was not going to waste anyone's time asking about past lives; I had enough to deal with concerning the one I was in.

CHAPTER 5

The Legacy

Finally I had broken through the barrier between worlds. This changed everything for my dad and a lot for me. Amazingly, my dad had received the message I sent him in exactly the way I had sent it. I felt empowered by the experience, and even my cup felt alive. It was a nice emotional complement to the peacefulness of this place. Besides Andy, my constant companion, there was a peaceful openness that lived in the core of my being, and now it felt more wonderful than usual.

But my teacher didn't look even a little pleased with my accomplishment, so I raced back to the grassy meadow, my place of comfort, with its small weatherworn boulders I could lean up against, sit on, or use as giant interactive notepads for my musings. Their stony surfaces were easy to manipulate, and because everything here is photon based I was literally creating photonographs with my musings.

Sitting on one of the small boulders, petting Andy, I felt like I had accomplished something very big and that if I could talk to my dad I could also talk to the rest of my family. Wanting very much to communicate with my mother, I checked to ensure that my emotions were all engaged, picked up my cup, and making sure my voice sounded exactly like my earth voice to avoid startling her, I said clearly, "Mom, I am okay, and I love you." But instead of clarity and connectedness, it was like playing telephone with a kid who was not holding the string taut enough to allow for the transmission of vibrations into his tin can. I tried several more times, but each was worse than the last. The life force that had emanated from the cup seemed almost completely gone, so much so that the hollow, empty tone that came back out of the cup had Andy barking.

I returned to my teacher to ask him what had happened. "I think I broke my cup. It doesn't work anymore," I told him.

He replied, in an unexpectedly compassionate tone, "Your cup is not broken, and you did not damage it. Your deep desire to speak with your mother comes from feeling that you have to rescue her."

"I don't understand. What is the difference between what I just did with my father and trying to let my mom know I'm okay and love her?" I asked.

"The exchange with your father was not about rescue but about assisting him with some choices. Your relationship with your father was one of equality while you were on earth, and you delivered your message from a place of love and respect. Your two souls were always equal and connected despite the fact that he was your parent and you were his child," my teacher replied.

"Yes, I never did feel the need to rescue my father on earth, but aren't I trying to rescue him now from his pain?" I replied.

"You responded to his pain, but you clarified something for him rather than acting out of a need to rescue him. Your relationship with your mother was one of deep love, but you had a fear. Do you know what that fear was?" my teacher asked.

"That if I didn't act the way she wanted me to she would take it personally?" I replied.

"You were conditioned to please her, but that is not quite it," my teacher answered.

"Many children are trained to please their parents," I pointed out. "Not out of fear that the parent is emotionally fragile," he replied. That made me remember the fear I had had from a very young age that my mom was going to die. I had nightmares about being left without her. Fearing for her mortality, I could not stand to see her upset or gone from the house. Accessing my father's memories reminded me of the many times I had panicked when she left me home to go out on errands. At such times, my dad could reduce my anxiety only if we went on a pseudo-search for her by walking around the neighborhood. Sure, my toddler self just wanted to be with her, but I also knew that being with her created comfort for her. I feared that she would not survive without me.

"Your relationship with your mother is very different from your relationship with your father, and your desire to rescue her will interfere with her ability to move forward on her path as well as with your ability to advance your own understanding. It is not your agreement to have this level of conversation with your mother at the moment."

While reflecting on my relationship with my mother, I panicked, imagining her to be on the verge of taking her own life as she was now so alone, without anyone to rescue her, and that it would be my fault if such an incident occurred. On one level, it is empowering to feel you are the center of another individual's world; but when distorted, this feeling creates a prison. I even sent a message to my dad asking him to promise to be there for her if she needed help. Later I came to understand that this had more to do with my relationship with her than with her lack of inner strength. I realized I had been trained to give her parts of myself to feed upon, to keep her from dying.

My teacher further told me my cup had momentarily seemed to lack life force due to my fear that I would displease my mother— a dynamic that had been central to our relationship. I had been afraid to even have a girlfriend, burdened as I was by the same feeling that if love is given, you owe something to the person who gives it to you. Because my mother's type of love demanded loyalty, I didn't know I had other choices. Through kindness and play, she made sure I was going to love her, for she feared losing me. She had never known love in her life until I was born. There was one girl who had been interested in me and with whom I had even exchanged my first kiss, and now I felt bad that I had pushed her away, given my new understanding of why.[1]

"I get this now, so can I still send word to my mom that I am okay?" I asked my teacher.

"You have never had a free conversation with her. The energy has to be clear to be love," he responded.

I wondered how to alter the dysfunctional patterns between my mom and myself to clear the energy. Certainly my behavior with her was subconscious as I was only a kid, but on some level I knew there was a problem because I was emotionally interacting with my mom as if I were still six years old. I checked in with myself to see how I would have reacted at twenty-five, and there was no change. I was still emotionally six years old. This meant my reactions to her were not just a function of my age, and that since they were about me it was up to me, not her, to shift the energy.

Using my new abilities to see more in my dimension in order to better understand human emotions, I followed some communications I remembered to their roots and even discovered the existence of parasitic entities that feed off of the dark side of human emotions. These misanthropic feeders are hungry ghosts from some other universe.

On earth, my dad had protected me from the seedier side of humanity, but now, facing it without him, I also observed how love gets distorted and draws in shadow energies. For example, people

---

[1] It had even been a cause for leaving my father's house. If I couldn't have a relationship, I didn't see why he should be able to have one.

who love their addictions have an attachment to something with no life force. One can be attached to an addiction, an object, an outcome, or even a pain. My soul was working with a pattern my mom's soul was working out, and as much as I wanted to influence it, I could see that was her journey, so I had to learn to love her as she was—where she stood.

At times I felt both anger and compassion when I saw what my mom understood love to be. For her, love still could not be given without subconscious strings attached, a pattern that leads to suffering. Given the awareness of this pattern, I wanted to know what it would have been like for me had I stayed in my body. I came to the sad realization that for many years I would probably have maintained the dysfunctional pattern of this family lineage, due to my misunderstanding of love. Ultimately, I might have cut off my relationship with my mother completely while destroying this pattern within myself.

Had I not passed, I also would have lived an isolated life for many years, because in not understanding love I would have rejected it. I am glad I didn't have to develop further in that direction, because living a life isolated from love is how doors to the shadow places open, presenting a never-never-land with much to discover but no one to share it with. It was time to change this pattern by going to the core of the problem—anything less would have been like painting over rust.

It took me some time to dissolve my fear about displeasing my mother and to regain peace within our relationship. Fortunately I was in a dimension in which such changes could happen. It turned out that my mother did not take her life and was able to move past her initial intense grief, although she still felt a sense of abandonment and betrayal. For my part, I released any need to revisit the pain caused by the destructive pattern in my lineage. So I am free and she is free, and I love her deeply, while clear of any need to love her.

My dad came to his own understanding of how he enabled this lineage and was able to break free of it. His path and mine became increasingly more aligned—mirrors of each other's in two different dimensions.

The challenge, I learned, is to not be angry with anyone for the issues they are working out, which is true compassion. Such patterns temper and clarify how one walks in the world. Even amidst the greatest tragedy we cannot ascribe blame, for there are deep agreements forged on a soul level to walk a particular path and ultimately to claim it as our own so we set free not only ourselves but also those who walk the path with us.

After looking at my family's patterns of behavior, I better understood my current responsibility to those I love: making sure love is more available than tragedy. Discovering this piece of the puzzle changed me forever. And the silver cup vibrated again with the flood of memories that surfaced in my search to understand myself.

@@ @@ @@

Editor's note: Like every parent whose child has passed, I have to trust that souls, in their divine wisdom, cocreate events that are in the best interest of all. I am glad Galen does not have to live out the dysfunctional patterns imprinted on his psyche and that there is no longer any agreement left with that lineage. Even so, I will always regret that it became necessary to leave his earth life to process these issues.

My hope was that my intelligent, talented, good-looking son could have fulfilled his dreams on earth. But I can also see that he will realize them through this book as well as its sequels, and through an even larger project of transdimensional cooperation and communication, the details of which have not yet been revealed to me. Although at this point I can only speculate about his future legacy, he was part of what Native Americans call the Seventh Generation, and I think his legacy lies with them and those that follow.

CHAPTER 6

In Andy's Eyes

Once again I enjoyed running in the sunlit meadow with Andy by my side, and basking on my warm rock where I could feel the love flowing to my mom, my grandmother, and the rest of my family. The insights I had about my family and the nature of grief and love gave me greater clarity, almost enough to see how the universe was organized—at least that was how it felt. There was no question I had more emotional peace, which, in turn, impacted my view of reality.

One day while watching Andy, I became curious about whether his life had been as complex as mine. On earth, Andy would have been seen as just a dog, without as much consciousness or intelligence as a human. But since everything at the dimensional station in which I now exist vibrates at the same frequency, how was it that I shared it with a dog, I wondered. A fantastic dog, but a dog just the same.

In my search for answers, I cradled Andy's head in my hands and rubbed behind his ears so I could steady him enough to look directly into his eyes. In those eyes I could see a deep richness, and a connectedness that has no descriptor in human language.

I focused on the energy in his eyes long enough to see that there was a pure being looking back at me. I then became certain that Andy was not just my canine companion but also someone who transmitted an expansive life force.

I started to feel very proud of my revelation, but was about to learn that just because I understood some things didn't mean I understood all things. I found it easy to look into Andy's eyes because I so loved the form Andy was in. I am naturally attracted to dogs, which is likely why Andy was chosen to be with me. He had the form of something that on the earth I had opted to take care of—a service dog. Andy knew how to get into every molecule of my body to integrate, support, and align, which was why he became such a powerful presence for me. If I called out to Andy, he would respond just as any dog would, wagging his tail, licking my face, and jumping up on me eager to play. Yet looking into his eyes I could see there was a completely different being inside.

I went back to my teacher with some trepidation because I had never really looked in my teacher's eyes. I'd only seen the reflection of my own self-image there, and though it took courage I slowly looked up at my teacher's face. But I could not see anything—not even my own face! I could focus on his voice, his form, his hands, but not his face. There was no bright light emanating from him interfering with my sight, or a shining halo or wings, as are often depicted in earthly illustrations of ethereal beings.

I realized then that I did not have what was required to see my teacher's face. I knew what a dog should look like, but in a sense I did not know what this teacher should look like.

"Why can't I see your face?" I asked my teacher.

"You *can* see my face—it has been there all along. You have relied heavily on your cup to bring up memories and information, but you have never moved out of the past into the experience you are having now," he replied.

I wondered if I had been able to see Matthew's face only because of my father's need to communicate. "But I still can't see your face," I insisted.

"Yes you can," he repeated.

I dropped my shoulders in discouragement, feeling like I was starting all over again learning about this dimension. For the first time since I had arrived in heaven, I cried, feeling like I would never understand how to function in the life I had now and that I would forever be living in the shadows of my memories. I returned to the grassy meadow and sat in frustration on my rock, which was no longer a source of joy because I didn't know if it really *was* a rock, and watched the sun rise and set for days on end. I just wanted to sit on my rock and think about where I was. I thought for so long that I eventually stopped dwelling on my frustration and feeling like an insignificant amoeba in a world beyond my understanding.

It was then that a space opened up in which I no longer questioned what was around me or had to use my imagination to project things into the open nothingness. In this space I was simply present, free of pretense and purpose. As children of the earth, we are taught to respond to stimuli around us so we know what to do with our bodies in any given situation, like members of the animal kingdom might do. The biological requirement of using a human body imprints itself on our identities; yet in this new place I found I could shed my human identity, including the connection to my cup and the grass of my meadow. I expanded past the horizon of the person I knew as Galen, and having done so, the fear that I was "less than" left me as well. Here I was pure spirit.

After a while I returned and was Galen once again, sitting on my familiar rock but with the awareness that I had found another level of consciousness. It seemed as if I had merged the spirit of who I was with the being known as Galen. I had gone to a place where I could connect to my spirit and call it back into who I knew myself to be. In doing this, I realized I was more than just human. To feel I existed, I no longer had to relate to the youth I had been or the family I had come from. I could just be.

I remembered my father had taught me about a space beyond what the mind knew, but at the time I had no frame of reference to comprehend what he was describing. Now this level of consciousness is as available to anyone in an earthly human body as it is in my dimension, because the spirit does not change from one dimension to another, only perception changes. Granted, this level of consciousness here is easier to access because here it is simple to take off all the outer layers of the self to get down to the truth of who you are. On earth, however, people use layers of identities and the defenses that go with them just to survive the fear in their midst, not unlike all the clothes they wear to avoid freezing. To survive attacks by predators, our ancestors had to be able to react quickly to their environment, and that fear is still ingrained in the human psyche, though being eaten is no longer a major risk; today it is expressed as fear of what is around the corner, over the edge, or under the bed. Many insane human behaviors have their origin in fear that was once required for survival and remains at the root of human nature. But it is possible to move past survival mode and into pure spirit.

I went back to my teacher and found that he looked like an ordinary human man, no longer larger than life but of normal height and proportions—more like Alec Baldwin than Alec Guinness (Obe-Wan Kenobi). When I looked in his clear blue eyes, however, I could see the same sense of expansiveness and knowledge I found in Andy's eyes, the knowledge of being a spirit having a personified experience. I wondered if my eyes now looked that way too. I had been afraid of seeing someone as completely connected to their spirit as my teacher, because I hadn't been able to relate to my own spirit yet. When I first arrived, my teacher's energy field made him seem larger than life, but as energy equalizes everything moves into perspective, and now my teacher appeared to me as having normal height and proportions.

Reflecting more on this level of consciousness, I became aware that some beings, such as the Dalai Lama, are so connected to their spirit that in their eyes you can see the circuit between soul, spirit, and matter completing itself. Such humans do not feel the need for fear or defensiveness, because they are no longer operating out of the biological imperative to survive but out of the spiritual imperative to love. They are spirits walking in flesh.

Truly, one does not have to leave the earth to understand what I now understood in my dimension. I realized that my initial sadness in this dimension was because of missing my spirit. One would have thought that I had it already, but that is not the case; it had taken until now for me to call my spirit back. It is because of being separated from their spirits that so many people on earth cry.

Even though this was a natural process, I had to wait for what seemed like a long time before I was given the opportunity to call my spirit back. It isn't a given that once you pass out of the body you are omni knowing. This dimension is no less a place of learning, no less challenging, than the earth plane.

Further, the number of years an individual has lived before passing, or whether the person was rich or poor, has no effect on the acquisition of knowledge and skills in this dimension. The only thing that gives someone an advantage here is if they loved deeply while on earth.

I returned to my rock with Andy at my side. We sat facing each other, and I looked deeply into his eyes again. This time I could feel myself being drawn into a clear liquid space while gazing at the beautiful spirit of this dog. I had no idea at that moment that I was looking into a portal.

Editor's note: Back on earth, the Assistance Dogs of the West decided to name their Student Achievement award after Galen and gave it to someone who had shown creativity training their dogs. I sat anonymously at the packed awards ceremony held at Santa Fe's renowned Lensic Theater, where Galen had once performed in an elementary school production and where we had seen *The Pirates of Penzance* with his grandmother years before. After the award was given, I quietly left the theater, virtually unseen and unrecognized.

All individuals must face the transition that death brings. Death itself is not the great equalizer; the great equalizer is the size of one's heart. Ultimately, I have concluded, the heart is reduced to either fear or love, and beyond a certain point they are mutually exclusive emotions, so that if you move forward in love you become naturally fearless and vice versa.

In my early thirties, I had a dream in which I was a senior detective in charge of hunting down a murderous sociopath. The story would have fit nicely into an episode of *The Twilight Zone*, for the unique feature of this dream was that there was not an ounce of fear in my whole being. It was as if it had been surgically removed, and having no fear anywhere in my emotional field provided an exhilarating euphoria.

It was my call in this dream whether or not to order the other officers on my team to open fire on the sociopath. The decision came quickly, but as I gave the order to fire at the monster I realized I had made a terrible mistake, because alive the miserable energy field that pervaded this criminal would be contained in his body, but if he were killed the pernicious vortex would be free to find a new home in that of another malcontent. I took it upon myself to locate the person who was now under its influence, and after spending what felt like months in search of this insidious energy field I found it in the body of a young boy.

Presented with another decision to make at this point, I did something that surprised me: I sent this boy as much love as I could. Then the dream ended—or so I thought. In my awake state I still had absolutely no fear anywhere in my psyche and felt as empowered and energized as I had been in the dream. I thought about how being fearless in the dream was great but meant nothing without putting love into action. About forty-five minutes later the euphoria of fearlessness started to fade, and I felt like my old self once again, but was I?

CHAPTER 7

Hitchhiker
in the Universe

Everything in our universe depends on balance with something else, and when the balance of one energy interacts with the balance of another portals and vortexes are created. It is no different from what happens when a cool air mass merges with a warm one, creating cyclostropic flow. Moving about in the available dimensional levels and layers is done using portals, not to be confused with tornadoes or revolving spirals like on the *The Time Tunnel*, a TV show from the 1960s. In a portal you travel at will, while a vortex, which tends to be larger, draws you along, generating an urgency to keep moving, not unlike the difference between a placid stream and a raging river. A portal simply allows you to be transported away from the environment where you are currently stationed, which is exactly what happened when I looked in Andy's eyes.

In a sense, this entire dimension is a portal because it is so easy to interact with one energy and then another. The matrix of this dimension allows for such interactive exchanges to take place, and unlike the earth's matrix, which is about polarity, here the purpose is to interact rather than compare things to each other so they are good or bad, black or white. Yet these two schools of learning fit together perfectly like the yin and yang symbols, meaning they are not really separate.

There were times when Andy wasn't around, which I had never thought much about, knowing that dogs like to go off and play, chase things, and visit others. But as I began to understand that things here are not what they seem to be, my perceptions shifted. And although I'm aware that there is no separation here and everything is available through a thought or feeling, sometimes when Andy was gone I wanted to know where he went.

I didn't need to connect to him if he wasn't there. The neediness and desire to call things in is simply not present here, as it is on earth. Here one is integrated with an environment in which everything is available. I thought this place was fantastic, but now I was feeling even more supported by the matrix that was in effect here; I could literally feel it and feel a part of it.

So one day with Andy sitting in front of me, I looked into his eyes and asked him, "Where exactly do you go when you are not with me?"

Somehow hoping there would be an answer, I started to feel my whole essence being pulled forward into a space where I lost all perception of my body and seemed to have no arms, legs, shoulders, or head. It was like fainting, but instead of losing consciousness and being engulfed in a vast sea of nothingness, I found my mind had stilled and my supra-consciousness had merged with Andy's essence, which looked nothing like I had expected.

I was enveloped in a beautiful aqua blue, semitranslucent sphere—like a protective force field that might envelop a character from a science fiction story, but I was the character and I could feel the protection of Andy all around me. What I looked like floating inside of Andy I did not know, because I had no hands or feet to hold out in front of me, but I assumed I too was a semitranslucent ovoid. We moved forward together, two spheres of light, one inside the other, which felt like going through a wormhole or tunnel of energy in which nothing existed until it *did*. Andy took me on a tour of many different dimensions where there were things I could see and relate to, some of which we could only peer into from the outside because they were reversed energetically. I saw beings of light and beauty, as well as others I felt an urge to repel away from, but always I felt safe in Andy's presence. That first experience with Andy was akin to visiting the cantina of the Mos Eisley spaceport on the planet Tatooine in *Star Wars*.

Because polarity is not operational in most of the life stations in our "multiverse," there is seldom a need to have symmetrical bipedal humanlike bodies. In fact, being human is not part of everyone's agenda, as most evolving conscious beings choose not to work with the human experience in the third dimension. They have their reasons for not doing so, just as others have their reasons for utilizing the human experience. One path isn't better than another; it is just different. Very advanced conscious beings can and do use the earth experience without even being in a human body. They come to accomplish something—to transmit an energy, teach, serve—and they walk, swim, or root among us, as the case may be, but are not less advanced than we are and are often far more advanced. Such highly developed beings in our midst are well camouflaged and wish to remain so. Only those humans who are intuitively open to certain energy fields perceive these beings.

Eventually, Andy and I returned to the position we were in before the trip, as if our experience had been only a daydream. "Ah ha!" I exclaimed with some jubilation. "You are no more a dog than I am. You are a dog because I expect you to look like a dog and act like a dog, but I know you are not really a dog. So you can talk to me now."

But Andy just looked at me, tilted his head and panted, holding on to the image of being a black lab. And I have to admit it was comforting that Andy just stayed a dog. He gave me exactly what I expected on one level and freedom on another.

Because he was so receptive and comforting energetically, and being with him was completely different from experiencing the paternal authority of my teacher, I realized that Andy was actually an experiential teacher. He wouldn't tell you, "Go look at this or consider that," but in merging with his energy you were taken along with it, though only as far as you expected or wanted to go. Andy may have been a dog on earth, but he was really an advanced conscious being who, for whatever reason, chose to be in a dog body for a time on earth and has chosen to be a teacher for me here. On earth he had no doubt been a teacher as well, but not in a traditional sense.

Those who trained Andy on earth would have recognized a dog that completely understood what was being said to him. Appearances on earth can be quite deceiving without external clues about who is a teacher and who is not, who is an angel and who is not. The energy field created by Andy's presence transmits a vibration that affects everyone around him, which is why he was such a perfect portal. Any human who had contact with Andy and was truly paying attention would have been drawn to travel. In truth, many sentient beings, including humans, are experiential teachers to whom you need only make a connection to feel the opportunity for learning.

Following my first trip with Andy to other dimensions, I took many more with him as my force field protector. He taught me how to move safely through the portals, how to stop, view, and when appropriate, interact with those of other dimensions. Many humans do this all the time in dreams, so transdimensional travel is not unique to the dimension in which I live. But for me, it is a conscious experience during which I have no concerns about needing to protect a material body. I know I am here to learn as much as possible, which is really the only difference between where I am now and living on earth, where many forget they are there to gain experience and learn how to interact with the world around them. The point of being on earth is not to outwit the environment or survive it, as if you were in competition with it, but to just be in life.

It was a while before I traveled transdimensionally by myself, because there were still many things I didn't understand. For example, in some dimensions, perhaps best described as "antimatter dimensions," the energy is reversed and therefore considered negative energy, but not because it is malevolent; it is just how energy is organized. Still, I am not designed to be in an antimatter dimension and would be annihilated in such a place. These antimatter dimensions maintain a balance and at the same time churn the energies to cause movement. So while there is no good Captain Kirk and evil Captain Kirk,[1] there may be a matter Kirk and an antimatter Kirk, for everything has a counterpart to keep the energy in motion in the grand cosmic spiral.

Eventually I did travel by myself to dimensions I had discovered with Andy, using various aspects of nature to find portals. For instance, I could look into a pool of water and find a portal, a grove of trees, or even a structure I created to find a portal. All around there are portals where one has access to other dimensions and "The Great I" itself. On earth these portals are also accessible. I was no longer restricted to level twenty-one, my arbitrary designation for this dimensional state, nor did I have to incarnate somewhere to experience other dimensions. As I learned later, the decision to return to experience another incarnation is a personal choice, and not something one has to do.

It was in a portal where I encountered the misanthropic feeders that must attach themselves to humans to survive on earth. This

---

[1] *Star Trek*, "The Enemy Within," season one, and "Mirror, Mirror," season two, original series.

they do by feeding off the energy of addictions and negative emotions such as fear, literally using the life force of humans as their force field to survive in a place they do not belong. They are attracted only to individuals who are disconnected from their spirits, and they further encourage that disconnection until the life force is gone. It was unpleasant to watch these feeders in action, but better to be aware of them than not.

It was amazing to see the great diversity of beings in other dimensions and observe how various life forms assume shapes to fit their dimensional worlds. Since most are not in realms teaching polarity, they either have asymmetrical bodies or, as in pools of consciousness, no bodies at all. I have started to experiment with directing my travels to certain places, such as the Orion or Lira star systems, and I have had great adventures doing this but cannot yet control my movements accurately enough to always arrive at designated destinations. I also cannot explain how it is possible to be anchored in one dimension and yet move through these expanding and contracting portals to travel around the universe any more than I can explain how this can be done in dreamtime. As my dad once told me, it is very similar to the way one can have an out-of-body experience and still have a solid body to return to.

There are times I encounter beings that want to hitch a ride in the portal I've opened up, but I don't always let them. Although I have met many pleasant beings that way, there were others with whom I did not want to associate and had to politely force them out of the portal. For the most part, however, it is a very civil universe, and if you just say, "I don't wish to travel with you," beings will step back. It's not like there is a battle of wills going on.

It was on the return from one of my journeys that I had a guest follow me back. This creature had the unusual ability to compact down into a very small fuzzy ball, so I didn't notice a golf ball–sized wad of lint when it attached itself to my pant leg. I didn't discover it until I was back at my rock and could feel its fuzzy weight on my leg.

The curious creature had the same warm energy Andy had, so as it expanded I let it wrap itself around my left hand and right arm. It could adjust its size to an impressive degree—with its head resting on top of my left hand, its tail draped over my right shoulder—and if stretched out all the way it would have been taller than I was on earth. It was soft and responsive to touch, brilliantly colored with every shade of the rainbow in its fuzz, and it had two googly eyes, like the toys with white outer circles and black inner ones that twirl around if you shake them. As it kept expanding out like a fuzzy slinky, I could see a large segment of bright green, another of bright opalescent purple, and yet another of sunshine yellow. Some sections had patterns in them like circles, triangles, or squares.

I later learned that Wyrme, as I called it because of its tubular shape, is nearly unique in the entire universe, with only a few such creatures in existence, and has been around for a very long time, living in a place where there is only now. When Andy returned to my side, he looked at Wyrme and then at me, and I could almost see a smile acknowledging that the pleasant energy of Wyrme was all right with Andy. Wyrme was everything one would want an alien companion-to-be, and it quickly figured out what energies would please me. If I hummed a tone, Wyrme would undulate in sync with it in a very entertaining way. When it contracted, it would move my arm in a beautiful fluid manner that brought me joy. It was actually emoting its feelings to me in its rhythmic contractions; but what was truly phenomenal was its ability to bilocate, which means I didn't need to move through a portal to bridge dimensions while in the company of Wyrme. The dimensions would just merge as if I were in two places at the same time. This being could ride on my energy field, but it didn't surf the wave—it was the wave. I felt this joyful, beguiling strange creature was somehow requesting to stay with me, and I saw no reason to send it back through the portal.

Editor's note: My head spins thinking about the implications of the being Wyrme. On a more mundane level, Galen fancied himself a magician in elementary school and left his trunk of tricks behind at my house. I knew he had a collection of about a hundred fuzzy wormlike things with googly eyes similar to his description of Wyrme. I placed them at the head of my bed so I could be thinking about Wyrme, and eagerly awaited hearing more about the role Wyrme would play in Galen's explorations.

Regarding Galen's other discovery, it was a big deal to him that I know about these etheric parasites, and he introduced them to me in a dream, up close and personal. After my dream visit, I realized I had encountered them before, but Galen didn't know that. The dream started off with Galen handing me a book to read about these beings. Now, I do not know how they see themselves, but it wouldn't surprise me if they modeled their appearance after that of their intended victims; be that as it may, to me they looked human. They gathered on the outskirts of human activity, and when I found myself in their midst I had the prevailing sense that they were organized like a religious cult.

These human-appearing beings were grotesque and unhealthy looking. Most were well advanced in years. They had firm cult-like rules to follow, and anything related to science or math was forbidden. They were not deep thinkers. I was recognized as an outsider, but for the most part I did not seem to be a threat to them. I was introduced to a few clan members and brought over to one—a man lying in a bed. His face appeared youthful until his aged arm came out from under the covers and forcefully grabbed my arm with the most unpleasant grip, whereupon his face suddenly shifted to that of a toothless old codger. He attempted to engage one of my chakras to drain energy from my body, but unlike some experiences I have had with these monsters in dream the attempt was somehow blocked. For this I was grateful, having had such creatures attempt to attach to me before, which was exquisitely painful, akin to getting kicked in the groin.

I observed how they traveled through their network of energy conduits that run just above the visible material of our dimension. And I observed them ensnaring a human victim by encouraging her to release control over her life, whereupon their gruesome tentacles of energy wrapped around her body so tightly that her features became distorted as the parasites sucked the life out of her ever so slowly. They had to work as a group since they could not snare a human one-on-one, hence the need for their cult-like regimens to control behavior.

Near the end of my visit to this hideout of transdimensional vampires, two new misanthropes arrived, a man and a woman who were more aggressive toward me as well as agitated by my presence. More evolved than the others at this nest, they were fully capable of attacking a human all by themselves. I backed away from their invasive overtures, raised my left hand at them, and using intention alone, dropped them in a heap on the floor.

Some younger members of the nest came over to me bearing a look that suggested they had never seen anyone single-handedly dispatch one of their members by the method I had employed. It was as if they wanted to ask me about it but asking questions was not their style, and that is where my visit came to an end.

A decade before Galen was born, seven individuals came together twice a week to be trained by an Egyptian adept for the sole purpose of helping those who were being overshadowed by these creatures. All hope is not lost if one is in their vice, but it does require a focused effort to become free of their entanglement and the assistance of those skilled at this energetic extraction. I had been invited to participate in the experiment, and our teacher said that if we succeeded we would be the first group in the Western world to engage in this kind of healing activity. But the inner work required of us was more than we were willing to commit to, and after a year the training sessions were canceled.

CHAPTER 8

Show and Tell

The dimension where I exist is as busy a place as earth. On earth there is a need to protect oneself when one's energy field happens to bump up against that of another, but here it is possible to go about one's business without interacting with others, although people often greet each other pleasantly, saying, for example, "Hello, good morning, and how are you?" People can be seen walking around everywhere, working on their own lessons and teachings, or even shopping, because some still like to shop and there are places where one can go and look at different wares and offerings.

My favorite places are the rooms in which many gather to attend classes. Looking exactly like they do on earth, some are small grade school—like classrooms with desks, while others are university-style lecture halls with stadium seating such as you would find in a planetarium. I sat in on one class that had well over two hundred people in it, whereas others have fewer then ten. You don't sign up for these classes or look on your schedule to see what you have been assigned, although the topics of the lectures are posted. For the most part, you are simply drawn intuitively to a particular classroom. Most of the students are humans from earth, because this is a dimension that many humans move toward. Those who are not earth humans are almost always humanoids from systems utilizing a lesson plan similar to that on earth. And although the class teachers here aren't the same as my personal teacher who met me when I crossed over, they are all wonderful, with distinct personalities and very different teaching styles.

There was a particular class I wanted to attend with Wyrme. It meant a lot to me that Andy did not see Wyrme as a threat, although I confess I was a little obsessed with the creature because it felt so good to be with it. I had even started to speak with Wyrme, which at first was not an easy task because all it seemed to instinctively care about was my emotional well-being, but I could not get it to understand my communication. Eventually, however, I began to sense that between its rhythmic pulsings was a type of communication, something I discovered when it crawled up to my head, nudged my left ear, and pulsed. Although this tickled, once I relaxed I started to sense thoughts present between Wyrme's pulses—not actual words, but a subtle greeting as understated as two strangers passing and nodding their heads ever so slightly. In this way I could listen to the being communicate its intentions, which was very much like learning Morse code with all its dots and dashes. As I continued to practice this type of communication with Wyrme, I found I could send information back.

By the time I took Wyrme to class with me, I knew how to make simple requests such as asking Wyrme to contract or move in a certain direction. There were also times when I needed Wyrme to leave me alone because I didn't always want a slinky, fuzzy being pulsing on my arm, and at such times it would comply with my request.

Wyrme seemed as curious about me as I was about it. As it studied my body, checking out how my skin or hair felt, I wondered if I was the first human Wyrme had ever come across. Part of my motivation in taking it to class was to give it a little more experience, so I requested it to contract so I could put it in my shirt pocket.

I arrived at class ahead of the teacher, who was to lecture on intention, which is about holding a particular belief or vibration so everything can run along that stream, much like beads move along the threads on which they are strung. This is not something unique to the earth plane but is operational in many dimensions. Without understanding intention, one cannot perceive the true nature of communication. On earth it is very easy to set an intention but equally easy to be distracted from it.

Thirty students, all of whom were from earth, were attending the class. Just like in classrooms on earth, some were reading and others were talking amongst themselves, but that all changed when an incredible-looking teacher came in. The teacher was over eight feet tall and, despite having arms, legs, and a head, was almost completely covered with a white flowing robe and a hood. Looking at the face of the teacher was like looking through an aquarium at fish swimming in the distance, giant kelp moving with the current, and other aquatic life forms making conscious choices about where they were going. The teacher's entire body had a lovely transparent sea-green color, from the exposed hands on up. There was no question this teacher evoked curiosity and stimulated one's imagination to consider what else lay underneath the robes and in what sort of environment the teacher lived. I wasn't sure what to make of the teacher's appearance. Here you can look any way you want to, but it requires an ongoing effort to hold a form that is not normally your own, so almost everyone uses the form they have been accustomed to using.

The teacher's name, Binai, gave no clue of gender. As Binai began to lecture on why intention was important to communication skills—transculturally as well as transdimensionally—Wyrme began to move out of my pocket; and while I attempted to pulse a request to stay still, the more Binai spoke about the significance of intention for communication, the more Wyrme moved and expanded. Normally when Wyrme expanded, it would still remain attached to some part of my body, but this time it plopped down to the floor and glided in front of Binai.

Suddenly, thirty rainbow-colored fuzzy tentacles emerged from Wyrme and connected with the arms and shoulders of the students, including myself. Almost everyone jumped out of their seats and attempted to pull the tentacles off them. Because I had never tried to pull Wyrme off, only then did I realize it had some way of adhering to the body, even though it had no suckers. I tried to calm everyone down by telling them Wyrme was a benign life form that meant no harm but it didn't help.

Binai raised both arms and brought them together in a loud clap, causing a visible shock wave to shake Binai's body like gelatin, and it expanded out, distorting space as it rippled throughout the classroom. Wyrme's rainbow-colored tentacles quickly retracted, and it curled into a small fuzzy ball as if shut down. I thought I was in trouble for sure, but the teacher just walked around the classroom reassuring the other students there was no danger. Then Binai continued with the lesson, but the students had lost their concentration and many silent queries were directed my way about what Wyrme was and where I got it. After class, as I was pelted with questions from many students, Binai walked over and informed me that my teacher wanted to see me.

I felt like I was being sent to the principal's office as I walked to my teacher's home nearby. When I sat down in front of him in his study, I could tell he was not angry with me, but he did have one eyebrow raised as if to ask, "What kind of mischief have you just created?" Then he put his hand out, and I knew what he wanted, so I reached into my pocket and placed Wyrme in his hand. Wyrme stayed compact and still, making me really curious about what Binai had said or done to stir it up and then calm it down again.

My teacher asked, "Do you have any idea what you have here?"

"I have no idea—it came back with me when I was traveling through portals. I call it Wyrme," I confessed.

My teacher's other eyebrow went up as he said, "You are traveling through portals?"

"Yes," I replied, "Andy has taught me how to move through portals."

My teacher nodded and said, "Okay, so you really have no idea what you have here?"

"None," I said.

"First of all, Wyrme is as good a name as any, because this is a being with no name." He explained that Wyrme is ancient. No one knows where it came from, and there are only a few in existence in the universe. When they appear, they are revered as magical.

"I didn't think there was anything magical. Magic is only a misunderstanding of where things come from or how they operate." Relieved that I wasn't in trouble, I fired off all the other reasons I could think of for why there is no such thing as magic.

"If I can get a word in, let me explain." Now it was my teacher who broke into a tirade as he pulled on his graying whiskers. "There is something called magic because magic exists unto itself. While the mind, science, and the universal laws and truths can explain just about everything in our various realities, there are still some beautiful unexpected occurrences that cannot be explained by any law or truth. For instance, there are magical beings in this area of the universe that are like glitter that keeps everything beautiful and surprising, for they do not follow the laws of our universe. This being is one of them."

My teacher asked me to explain in more detail how I encountered Wyrme. "So, just how did you come to be with this?"

I told him how I had simply found it attached to my jeans, with no idea where it came from, and I described how I had interacted with it since then, trying to communicate with it and having some success getting Wyrme to understand my requests.

Looking surprised, my teacher commented, "As we teach, all things come from Source, from 'The Great I,' but there is reason to believe that this being did not come from Source. We have had many discussions about this being." He looked admiringly at the ball of rainbow-colored fuzz in his hand, and continued, "This is a being that can likely exist both in matter and antimatter, but no one knows for sure because we cannot follow it. Earth humans work with polarity, but this being bridges polarity and likely traveled with you because it has a certain curiosity about those who work with polarity. That curiosity comes with a price, however, as such beings are very alluring, causing people to become obsessed with them to the point of losing their will. Do you find yourself unable to be without this one?"

"No," I replied emphatically. "In fact, there are times I don't want Wyrme moving about on my body." It pleased my teacher to hear this, because it meant I was not addicted to Wyrme. "When I don't want it on me, I just make a request that it contract, then put it in my pocket or set it next to me on a rock. But it never seems to want to be on the ground."

"There is a reason for that," my teacher explained. "For it to integrate with this dimension, it can't be too far away from a being with a pulse, a circulatory system, and a nervous system. It feels alone when it is limited to contact with only light bodies, so it seeks the company of those who have a certain physical form, which is why it feels so much like a pet. But do not be fooled by its size—it can expand to such an extent that it could cover a whole planet."

"So why did it reach out to all the students in class?" I asked.

"Likely it could not help itself, as it has a strong need to connect to inquiring beings who have pulses, so it was drawn instinctually toward everyone. In the classroom of intention where everyone's

curiosity was piqued and their minds were open. Wyrme undoubt-
edly felt compelled to feel the pulses of all beings present who
held the intention of learning."

This made me think back to the journey I had been on when
Wyrme attached to me. Curious and full of wonderment about
everything, I must have been a magnet for the being. I guess when
one is open and full of the joy of learning, magic just comes naturally.

"Have such beings ever visited the earth?" I asked.

"Many times, and in some cultures they were, and are still are,
revered. This is the rainbow serpent of the Australian Aborigines,
the Chinese rainbow dragon, and Quetzalcoatl of Mesoamerica.
But they don't visit now as they once did. If you thought the chaos
in your classroom was bad, imagine the fear and panic on earth if
one of these beings revealed itself. If they go to earth, they remain
small and inconspicuous," he replied.

"Is it all right that I have Wyrme then?" I asked, hopefully.

My teacher kept admiring the creature in his palm, as if it
were a large gem from one of the Smithsonian museums, and said,
"It is a lot of responsibility, because in many ways you do not have
Wyrme, Wyrme has you, and you may find one day it will be gone
as quickly as it came. But this magical being has chosen to work
with you as a companion, and you seem to be balanced with it. It
also seems to be learning a great deal from you. Do understand,
however, it can take you to dimensions that do not serve you.
Therefore, be very clear in your communication with it and learn
to say yes and no before you travel with it."

Out of concern that I had already pushed my teacher's patience
with the day's events, I did not tell him I had already been traveling
with it, and just answered, "Okay."

I headed back to my favorite rocks with Wyrme in my shirt
pocket, but it bothered me that the whole time my teacher had it
in his hand, Wyrme had remained an inanimate fuzzy ball. Upon
arriving at my grassy hillside, I set the little fuzzy ball on a nearby

rock. It looked just a little gray, and the fuzz felt a little stiff, making me worry that I had damaged this rare creature of the universe.

I sent out the thought, "Open up," but nothing happened. "Welcome back," I said out loud. Still it did not move. I then thought about how incredible it was to have met one of these unique creatures from a universe in which there is a surprise around every corner and learning opportunities that provide great renewal. Without realizing it, I was beaming gratitude for what Wyrme had helped me learn—that it is truly a beautiful thing to keep one's imagination open. Suddenly I thought I saw a faint pulse in the fuzz. In response, I sent waves of gracious appreciation and love back to Wyrme, the same energy Wyrme had been sending me all along, whereupon Wyrme started to unwind and expand. I felt good that my efforts were actively putting some life back into it and that I was able to participate with it in the same way it had with me.

Wyrme expanded out on the rock, stretching as if it were a cat waking up from a nap. Then it looked me in the eyes and said, "Thank you," in tones clearly audible for the first time—a new form of communication with this magical creature, pleasing me no end.

෨෧ ෨෧ ෨෧

Editor's note: After hearing about Galen's experiences in classes, I asked what determined the nature of the experience the other students in his class had had after they crossed over. He told me this depended on how much effort was required to integrate into the new dimension and on the belief system they had on earth. For example, people who strongly believed that upon passing they would be surrounded by the classic heavenly environment with

Galen, age sixteen, overlooking the Rio Chama in northern New Mexico, on his last hike with his father. This vista evokes the landscapes Galen explored when he first integrated with his new dimension.

Galen, age two, playing in front of Pasadena City College.

Galen, age four, posing on an overlook of Los Angeles.

Galen, age eleven, with his grandmother Adele and his father, awaiting a performance of Pirates of Penzance *outside Santa Fe's Lensic Theater.*

Galen, age eleven, and his father.

Galen, age fifteen, acting in a production of Godspell.

Andy, the noble search and rescue dog who befriended Galen almost immediately upon his arrival on the other side.
PORTRAIT BY CHRIS KELLY.

winged angels playing harps would likely not be disappointed, but neither would they be at Galen's particular station. As individuals become more integrated into this new dimension, however, they experience things according to vibration rather than belief. Belief helps teachers and guides assist individuals, but vibrational level ultimately determines how they are organized into different schools and locations.

CHAPTER 9

Woman in the Window

So Wyrme had a voice! This was exciting because I had tried to get Andy to speak as I knew he could, but seeing him hold his Labrador form so well with those beautiful, loyal eyes, I'd given up trying. With Wyrme, not only could I send intention, I could actually hear a real voice! I immediately struck up a conversation with Wyrme, saying, "Oh, you can talk! Is it all right that I call you Wyrme?" But Wyrme just gave me a blank stare. Since its eyes had no depth, I couldn't really look into them and wondered if there was no twinkle or inner communication that eyes normally hold because this being didn't belong to any dimension or hadn't even come from Source.

Clearly Wyrme was a conscious being, but what it was and how it functioned were questions I pondered as I watched it continue to come back to its normal color and shape. I sent Wyrme more gratitude, love, and appreciation, but all it did was coil up a little and purr because it was so pleased I was sending it such feelings. I suppose if it were a dog it would have rolled over to have me scratch its tummy as this point, but still it would not converse with me.

Finally, I stood over it and said, "I know you can speak, so I command you to speak to me!"

Wyrme looked at me with puzzlement, since I had never commanded it to do anything before. Wyrme lifted itself as if it were a puppy wanting to be picked up. I am now embarrassed to admit that I ignored its overture and it changed back into a little fuzzy ball looking almost pitiful on the rock with only the wind moving its fuzz around. So I picked Wyrme up and brought it close to me, gently blew just hard enough to move the fuzz around, and my coaxing worked. Wyrme expanded, sprung onto me with joy, rubbing my ear and curling around my neck just like a puppy might do. I continued to be puzzled, however, and wondered how I could get it to speak to me again.

The day's events had tired me out. I require sleep just like everyone else does, even though I don't lose consciousness—my body simply goes into a state of repose. So I dropped down on the grass with my head resting against the rock, and Wyrme curled around my neck like a muffler pulsing out a kitten-like purr. While asleep, I thought I could hear Wyrme speaking with me. First I heard, "Hello, Galen." I later learned that Wyrme likes to follow a very formal protocol in conversation, but there was a slight problem as I was hearing a mixture of earth languages, including English, Chinese, and Spanish. When the voice spoke in Spanish there were certain words I could pick up, and I swear at times it sounded like Klingon (à la *Star Trek*), but always the voice was soothing and comforting.

In my conscious dream I could also see Wyrme moving in a new way in front of me, exactly the way a Slinky travels—in end-over-end somersaults—something I had never observed before as it had always ridden on my shoulders or in my pocket. I followed it down a hallway until it came to a door, where it tapped three times, causing the door to swing wide open. Wyrme tilted its head, gesturing for me to look through the doorway, where I saw a collage of the most beautiful images I had ever seen of star systems, galaxies, and nebula, but unlike the static images from the Hubble space telescope, this vista was alive. Wyrme looked up at me with its flat black eyes, and I could sense its intention was to show me this incredible space scene. My guess was that if I walked through this doorway I would fall into the stars, but I didn't want to test my theory.

Wyrme spoke again, using words from many languages I could not understand, but through the gibberish I was able to sense most of what it was trying to say because it illustrated its intention using the starscape I could see through the doorway. Wyrme had the ability to connect two points of energy, regardless of how far apart they were or in what dimension, and then fold them together to create a bridge between them. I recalled a physics class explanation of how two points at opposite ends of a piece of paper can be brought together by folding the paper, which was exactly what Wyrme was doing, using these breathtaking space vistas as its palette. Wyrme didn't have to travel through the portals I had been working with but could just appear wherever it wanted to in its multidimensional universe of its own volition. Wyrme was the ultimate example that size does not matter.

When I woke up, I found Andy sleeping by my side and Wyrme purring on my chest. I contemplated why I could hear Wyrme speaking only in dreamtime, why it was so clear in one level of consciousness but not another. Obviously, bullying Wyrme only insulted it while kindness and gratitude prompted it to communicate on many levels. My teacher had said no one knew what Wyrme really was, but maybe no one had bothered to ask Wyrme or knew how to ask. Sure, everyone seemed to be in awe of it, but to me it was just a little fuzzy thing with a lot of curiosity and love to share.

As word had gotten around that I had Wyrme, there was no need to hide it, and I would allow Wyrme to drape itself around my shoulder like a jungle cat on tree branches. Of the many individuals who came to see it, few wanted to touch it, as if a rumor had circulated that once it attached you wouldn't be able to get it off. But I let people know that with their permission Wyrme would touch them, and Wyrme thrived on these encounters. It was like having a snake wrapped around you that everyone is too scared to touch but at the same time can't keep their eyes off its innate beauty. I have to admit I enjoyed the attention just a little. Before Wyrme came into my life, I had privacy and I liked it—I was always aware of everyone else, whether they were on a hillside reading or walking and chatting together in small groups—so still it was a bit disturbing to trade my peaceful anonymity for the celebrity-type energy that had descended upon me. It got to the point where Wyrme would even look around to see if there was someone up ahead that it would like to attract. That is how much it liked the spark of everyone's emotions as they gave it attention.

No wonder these creatures had visited the earth in ancient times, I thought. I could imagine their delight from the attention throngs of earthlings would heap upon them as they descended from the sky in some dramatic way. People wanted to know if Wyrme could talk, and I tried to explain how to encourage it to do so, but no one could do it successfully so they just settled for gushing and fawning over Wyrme, or petting it to make it purr. One time I saw Andy sort of roll his eyes at this, and I could tell he was thinking, Oh no, not again.

On occasion it would see someone up ahead and try to hide, which I found a little funny. I could not figure out at first why Wyrme did not want connection with certain individuals, because everyone at this dimensional level has the same energy field, with good intentions and no malice. When it wanted to hide, it would attach itself to the back of my head and shoot itself down my spine, which felt funny. It was not that anyone was unpleasant, but if they were still processing a lot of loss or grief that Wyrme did not want to experience, it would divert itself away from these vibrations.

Of course, I had my moments of sadness in my own processing but was never lost in indentifying with them.

On one of my walks with Wyrme and Andy in tow, something unusual took place. I had stopped under an apple tree and started eating an apple. In this dimension I eat for the pure enjoyment of it, not because I have a body that requires food, and even have take-out Chinese when in the mood, though of course, all foods derive from my memory. I was appreciatively pondering my connections to the apple I was munching (I have learned to be present in the moment with whatever it is I am doing) when Andy sat up at attention because of something behind me and Wyrme shimmied down off of my shoulders, tapped me on the chest, and gestured for me to look.

As I turned around I saw, ten paces directly behind me, a forlorn-looking woman floating in the air, behind a rectangular window. The slow undulations of her hair, gown, and scarves gave the impression that she was submerged in water. She wasn't "dead," but neither did she look healthy. I had never before seen someone in this dimension who showed any sort of weakness. Startled, I jumped to my feet and walked toward the window. As I advanced, the window retreated, maintaining the ten-pace distance between us. This was frustrating because the woman behind the window looked distressed and in need of help. Wyrme tightened itself around my neck, as if trying to pull me away from the image, and even Andy stood between the window and me as if to block my way. It became clear that my only option was to just watch the image, which soon got smaller as if it were moving off into the distance, until it popped out of sight. "What was that?" I asked Andy.

Wyrme and Andy just looked back at me, acting as if they had never seen anything like this. While we walked to my house nearby, I heard a popping sound and the same woman appeared directly in front of me. Andy was not as startled this time, but despite his curious and explorative nature watched cautiously two steps behind me, while Wyrme tapped my chest as if to caution me. At that moment little windows started to form around the woman, and as they got larger I could see that each enclosed a different environment and people. In one window there was a scene of snow blowing hard in a blizzard, and in another there was a desert-like scene so dry that a man looked dusty.

Unable to get closer than the ten-pace distance, I could sense that the people in the scenes all looked as distressed as the woman in the largest window. As quickly as they had popped in they would pop out, and feeling perplexed by this phenomenon I returned to my teacher's residence.

I knocked on the door, but there was no response. I could feel that my perceptions of everything were being disrupted. I had always had access to someone who could answer questions, even if I just dropped by the school and found a teacher—but not now.

I made my way home, doing my best to avoid looking at the sky in case more windows popped into view. I decided to just wait for whatever was causing the unusual visitations to pass, as my experience had been that in this dimension things never stayed out of kilter for long. I plopped on my bed, figuring it was the best place for me to wait out this event and let it blow through like a summer storm. Wyrme cuddled around my neck, but it was not purring as before and behaved more like a fawn that protectively lies down on the forest floor because it senses something ominous is present. Even Andy had one eye open watching the door from his position on the couch next to my bed. I did my best to just relax and remain alert without concerns about my environment.

In this calm, clear space, I found I could talk to Wyrme again. I asked, "What is going on?" Wyrme, excited to have this communication link restored, spoke rapidly in many languages until it calmed down enough to change to English, with the hint of a British accent. Because I am human, Wyrme seemed to expect me to be able to understand any earth language, but since I couldn't it had to try out a few dialects before arriving at one I could comprehend.

After it began speaking English, it made me start the conversation again with formal greetings. Now I was the one rolling my eyes as I said, "Good afternoon, how are you?"

"I am well. How are you?" Wyrme responded.

I do not know how Wyrme developed this communication etiquette, but I had to comply with the formality and slow down the pace of my words if I wanted to hold a conversation. "I am fine, thank you. It is a pleasure to speak with you," I continued.

After we dispensed with the ritual of greeting each other properly, I asked, "May I ask you a question?"

"Of course you may," answered Wyrme.

"What was that we were just experiencing?"

"Oh yes," Wyrme said, "the windows. I have already shown you that time and space can be folded to bring them together. Because of who I am, these windows open up and follow me, as they enclose individuals who want to transport from one dimension to another, but it is not my place to accommodate them."

At this point Wyrme became so excited it lapsed into several other languages, so I figured this was a hot topic. When Wyrme calmed down again and returned to intelligible English, it told me that there are beings who get lodged in these dimensional boxes of reality because they die before their time, usually violently and always by their own hand.

"Such a death confuses the sequence of events, but they do something to disrespect their lives and it creates confusion," Wyrme explained. "These beings are drawn to anyone who can change the circumstances in which they are imprisoned, and they will travel through time and space in their quest. They are attracted to me because I move through dimensions quite easily and freely, but it is not my place to assist them."

I understood what Wyrme was talking about because even though my passing was due to a violent accident, preparation had been in place. There was an agreement, and I was expected.

"No wonder these individuals look distressed—they were suicides," I said.

"But not always intentional suicides," Wyrme added. Curious if the floating woman had drowned herself, or the man in the snowstorm had wandered drunk from some tavern and died in the snow, or whether the dusty man had been banished from his tribe and died in the desert, I wondered if I had been drawn to them because I had a personal history of wanting to help someone in my family who was depressed and lost. I now understood why Andy and Wyrme were trying to keep me back from the windows; they could sense my attraction to them was not coming from a clear place in my psyche but was a reaction to my past.

Wyrme continued, "They are attracted to me because of what I can do, but I don't feel called to assist them." I had always understood Wyrme to be compassionate and nurturing, and it seemed a rather cold contradiction to hear Wyrme say it was not his place to assist the people in the windows. But at the same time, I know one cannot serve if it is not their place to serve, and I suppose it is possible that freeing the people from their imprisonment could put them in greater peril than leaving them there. I wondered if these individuals were the ghosts who sometimes make themselves known on the earth plane, unconsciously seeking someone to help unlock the energy field in which they are trapped. I asked Wyrme what could help them.

"I do not know, which is why I cannot assist them," Wyrme replied.

But just because a magical creature that vaultes time and space doesn't know how to assist these trapped beings doesn't necessarily mean that no one knows, I thought. I pondered how the people in the windows could be helped, but I had learned from my own family that sometimes this means doing something on a completely different level—giving the individual love and support where they stand instead of trying to rescue them.

"Thank you very much for speaking with me," I said, even bowing, as I ended the conversation with Wyrme on a formal note.

"Oh, I am very pleased to do so. Please converse with me again," Wyrme replied.

Walking outside, I found that everything had been realigned and the world was once again sunny and beautiful. So I returned to the home of my teacher, who was now there, and explained my experience, including what Wyrme had said to me about the individuals in the windows.

He remarked, "Often this is the proper place for them, depending on what happened to them and what situation they are coming from. Thank you for reporting this to me, because not everyone sees these beings. Some of the teachers do, and if they are able to catch any of the windows as they arrive in this dimension, they can find a guide who can work with the individuals involved. It sounds like the woman floating was coming through the strongest, so likely the time is now for her to be helped."

"How long has she been there?" I asked.

"It has been five years since she drowned herself as a result of hopelessness and depression, but had she sought out assistance through the proper channels she would have received it. Suicide can be quite an egotistical experience. A certain maturation of energy needs to take place within her before she can be freed. I have sent word to the other greeters to be on the lookout for her so she can be released from her container, because that is what these beings are in—a dimensional container."

"What about the others?" I said.

My teacher asked, "Did they ever come as close to you as she did?"

"No, they were held back in the distance," I answered.

"Then it is not their time yet, and they will have to wait," he replied.

"What about people who smoke cigarettes and know full well it will cause a premature death?" I asked.

"That is a situation in which there is time to prepare the doorways."

At this point I realized why approaching the woman's window had caused it to back up: I was not the one meant to release her regardless of my compassion or desire to relieve the suffering I could feel coming from her. One really has to understand the circumstances under which one can serve. In this case, I could serve only by being a bridge to my teacher, who put the alert out so this woman whose time had come would be helped. I also realized that when I sensed things being out of alignment and couldn't find a teacher to talk to, it was my heightened anxiety about the windows that had made the teachers inaccessible to me. So it wasn't that my teacher was not at home; he is always "at home." I just couldn't access him. Holding an emotional state that is not clear and centered does not allow one to function properly at this dimensional station.

Once again Wyrme had brought me an experience that deeply connected me to my present, past, and future. There is no separation between times, and everything is, as the teachers often say, a spiral, in which what comes around goes around to create proper alignment.

◎ ◎ ◎

Editor's note: Interestingly, when Galen was seven or eight years old, I had a dream relating to the consequences of suicide in which I walked a pimply-faced teenager with stringy shoulder-length hair to a gray, nondescript beach. The sky was dull, and dark green water lapped up on the shoreline with waves no taller than two inches. By the time I sat this young man down on the sand, I became aware that that he had overdosed on drugs, though not intentionally. In the distance I could see many people who had come to greet him, but they were in a different reality, across a small inlet of water on a beach full of sunshine and rainbows, setting up a picnic table. They happily waved to us, I returned the wave but my gesture was to wave them off, because I knew the teenager, after disrespecting his life and ending it even if he had not consciously intended to, would have to wait a certain amount of time until he could join the others on the sunny side of the beach. This was not a punishment, but simply following the way things work in the universe. I have come to understand that the other side is not one dimension but multilayered and the one on which you find yourself has to do with experience, belief, and vibration, as Galen has already pointed out.

If indeed I, or my supra-consciousness, was assisting this young man, obviously his case was not as extreme as those Galen saw in the windows. But just like it takes preparation to integrate into the earth dimension (conception, development of the embryo, fetus, and so forth), the same holds true for the other dimension. Circumstances are different, but the pattern of "As above, so below" remains the same. Some say this pattern is chaos, but then, what is chaos other than formless energy trying to find form.

After getting the information from Galen about how suicide is viewed in his dimension, I pondered my views on the subject. As a physician I view assisted suicide or easing the passage of an individual who is dying with dignity, as compassion in action, for it serves no one to have undue pain and disability at the very end of life. This happens privately in hospitals all over the world, even if it just means increasing a morphine drip beyond the level compatible with being able to breathe. It is neither suicide nor murder, but as a society we need to develop rules and parameters for those in the throes of a terminal illness who choose to end undue suffering. It is not against nature to want to exist with dignity, but it is against nature to impose one's beliefs upon others. Once we mature past that point, maybe we can have consensus on what the end of life rules and parameters should be.

CHAPTER 10

Kid Brother

As it had been a while since I'd had an opportunity to create an enjoyable space for relaxation, I decided to take a hike on the trails of Bandelier National Monument, northwest of Santa Fe, a place I create through memory, accessible with the aid of the template of the real location. I put a red bandanna around Andy's neck, so he would look sporty, and prepared myself with a walking stick and backpack. I took Andy and Wyrme to the park entrance and then the Main Loop Trail, which is an easy scenic walk through the canyon past many archaeological sites, such as a Native American longhouse and several kivas.

Not long after beginning the hike, I heard a shuffling noise behind me, but when I turned around I saw nothing. I am getting pretty good at manifesting, so I thought maybe it was one of the park's Albert squirrels, but Andy didn't react. As we continued on, every once in a while I heard something behind me but when I turned around there would be nothing, and since my companions were not giving me any clue that I should be alarmed, I shrugged it off. As I was creating the experience I was having, I was not in any danger on this hike, but I wanted to fully engage with the sense of hiking free of distractions, observing the path I was on and enjoying the environment I encountered, just as I had tried to do on earth. This is always a very physical experience for me. Here my body may be made up of photons rather than elements on the Periodic Table, but it is no more an illusion than the human body, made up as it is of carbon, hydrogen, and oxygen. When I have an experience, I am not pretending to have one. The laws here are different, I don't have to respect the law of gravity that is in effect in the third dimension, and serious physical injury does not occur here—but there is still a physical body that needs to be attended to.

After a while, I turned onto a trail requiring a little more skill, the Cerro Grande Route, which is two miles one way up to Cerro Grande Peak, the highest point in the park at over 10,000 feet, so I could see the vistas. About halfway to the peak I heard a voice cry out, "Help!" accompanied by the noise of small rocks tumbling. I knew for sure now that somebody was behind me. Andy rushed back down the trail barking. While Andy pointed and barked, delighted to again be doing the job he had been trained to do on earth, I descended the trail a little way and found, tangled in the branches of a bush, a boy who appeared to be about eight years old.

As I picked the boy up and dusted him off, I realized he was dressed exactly the way I was dressed, had somehow created a crocheted rainbow-colored Wyrme that was pinned to his arm, and was holding a stuffed black bear with a red bandanna tied around its neck. Instead of crying, the boy looked up at me with a big smile and said, "Hi, I am so glad to meet you."

"Have you been following me?" I asked.

"Well, yes. I've wanted to meet you for a while, and I just haven't had the chance to do it. Today I saw you prepare for this hike, so I decided to come too," replied the boy.

"Do you have parents here?" I asked, trying to determine who was responsible for him and if he was lost.

The boy looked at me and answered, "No. I don't have any-body here." Then he added excitedly, "Is that Wyrme? Can I touch it?" I could tell I wasn't getting the full truth as he kept diverting the conversation away from what I was asking. Finally I was able to get him to reveal that his first name was Carl, although he would not tell me his last name. I didn't want to continue back up the trail because Carl was having a hard time with it, so we walked down together to the Main Trail Loop, where we sat down and I showed Carl Wyrme to appease him, with the hope that he would go back home.

"How did you come to be here, Carl?" I asked, hoping to learn anything that might help me understand who he was.

"I followed you here, don't you know?" Carl said.

"No, I am asking about this dimension. How long have you been here?"

"I don't know how long I have been here," he responded, without divulging more.

"How did you come to be here?" I asked.

"All I remember is that I was really sick and my mom was crying, and then I was meeting my teacher, who gave me this," said Carl, holding up his little silver cup, "and I have been going to my classes ever since."

Although Carl didn't seem to have a lot of experience at this dimensional station, everyone here was pretty much at the same level of maturity. But I didn't remember ever seeing a child this young among those I had met. I wondered if there was a special area here where those without much experience lived, and I was con-cerned that he might have wandered away from where he needed to be. We continued our hike back out the Main Loop with the intention of going to my teacher so I could get more information about Carl.

When Carl realized we were leaving the canyon, he started to fall behind and got upset. "Is anything wrong?" I asked him.

"You are going to take me back, but I don't want to go back," he replied, grabbing my hand. With this simple act, I was downloaded an incredible collection of images and a profound sense of innocence that expanded my whole universe. Although Carl looked like a child, he was clearly a very progressed individual with a highly developed sense of intuition and understanding. I shook my head at learning the same lesson I had learned over and over in this dimension, that things here were not as they appeared.

"Look, let's go see if we can find your teacher or your family," I said, determined to discover where Carl belonged.

"You are my family," the boy answered. "You are my big brother."

His intent declaration caught me off guard. I had no recollection of there ever being another child in my family, but he said it with such sincerity I had to check my memory to determine if there had been any mention of another child. I decided that Carl just needed to feel safe, and replied, "Okay, I will be your big brother."

"You *are* my big brother," Carl corrected me.

I walked hand in hand with Carl to my teacher. With Wyrme on my shoulder and a little crocheted Wyrme on Carl's, and with Andy on my left side and a black toy bear under Carl's right arm, we were mirror images of each other, only one short and one tall. Surprisingly, as we entered my teacher's study he said, "Hello, Carl, how are you today?"

"Hi, I am doing fine. Look, I found Galen!" Carl replied excitedly.

My teacher looked at us and smiled and then said, "Yes, I see you have finally met each other."

"Carl thinks I am his big brother," I said, feeling like the odd man out.

"You *are* his big brother," my teacher stated, explaining that when one comes to the earth plane there are many agreements so that success is assured in experience as a soul and a spirit. "Before you incarnated on earth, you were similar to what you are now— in a teaching dimension that allowed you to work out every possibility. Within your cup are all the experiences you have gained from your life on earth, which come back together to help you create the next experience," my teacher said.

"Are you talking about reincarnation? I asked.

"That is what it is called on earth. We just call it evolution, where soul and spirit continue to incarnate for experience. There are many combinations created, and no matter which one you choose, everything will successfully teach what you are intended to learn. In one of those combinations, you had a younger brother who would have idolized you and learned a great deal from you and from his father and mother. The soul you see here as Carl had an agreement to come into your family; but because life is always changing according to choices being made by others around you, Carl didn't end up in your family. Just because Carl was not part of your physical family, however, didn't mean he was cast off, because Carl has his combinations of possibilities as well. And so, he has come to be your younger brother in your spiritual family. You can't remember him from your conscious experience, but you may recall wondering what it would be like to have a younger sibling, indicating that the idea existed in your desires even if it didn't manifest in the experience you had. Ultimately, Carl incarnated into another family, where he was deeply loved and still has two sisters and a mother on earth. In this particular family, Carl became sick, and he passed at the age you see him now."

I looked over at Carl, who had lowered his eyes. "It is okay. My mom is okay, but I always wanted a brother," he blurted out.

Carl didn't have a lot of experiences in his cup except for knowing love and having a deep family connection, which I suppose made it easy for him to bond with me.

I felt compelled to ask where this had taken place, because it seemed I should have sensed we had something more in common than what I was picking up from him.

"Carl was brought up in Minnesota," my teacher answered.

Given that we were from the same country, I felt that there should have been something about his experience that resonated with me during my time on earth. "When?" I asked, still trying to understand the connection.

"Carl passed in 1954," my teacher explained.

"That's the year my father was born. I don't understand. He could not be my younger brother in the 1990s if he was born in 1946," I said, astonished. I sat down in a nearby armchair to steady myself.

"Earth utilizes linear time, but the soul does not. Carl was not sent back, from the soul's perspective. There is progression of universal time, but Carl's soul had never utilized twentieth-century earth before—any decade would have been a time progression from the previous earth incarnation. The soul sought out the best circumstance to maximize the experience it needed to progress and best serve those around Carl once it became clear he was not going to be in your earth family at the end of the century," my teacher further explained.

"Carl has been here for more than fifty years?" I asked incredulously.

"By chronological time, yes; but as you know, this dimension does not operate by earth time. Do you know what time it is on earth when you go through a portal or attend a class?"

"No, of course not," I conceded.

"Chronological time is very different from universal time, which is a spiral. This is well understood by earth physicists, but for everyone else it is confusing, because one hour is supposed to follow another. Spiral time is much more like the game Chutes and Ladders, where you can step across bands of time rather then just follow a fixed spiral."

"Okay, why don't I see children Carl's age in the places where I have been walking?"

"It's true, Carl's experiences are a little light for this dimensional station, but Carl's need to meet you was so heartfelt that he connected, and his talent at being intuitive and his strong belief manifest in some powerful ways. Carl had to meet you," my teacher revealed with a wink, which was a surprise given I had yet to see him even smile at me, let alone throw me a knowing wink.

"He had to meet me?" I asked.

"Galen, everyone's life holds many possible combinations of experiences," said my teacher, for the first time calling me by my name, "and for the soul, having an experience is success and learning from experience is invaluable. The time had come for you to know that you had a strong agreement with this little brother, who would have changed the course of life for many had that become his path. Ultimately there is still a deep agreement to work through with Carl, and at a future time, when you are both ready, you will be born as twins to provide many further possibilities for experiences together."

I sat in silence for a moment as my cup started to vibrate. I contemplated the many possibilities there are for experience in life and how fate is not what people think it is—predetermined parameters with limited opportunities. Then I stood up, and my teacher nodded at me. Looking at the boy, I said, "Come on, Carl. Let's go do something."

Carl doesn't stay with me all the time, but visits every once in a while from what I call level seventeen and I occasionally visit him. Here you can easily visit and connect with others as if you were visiting an aunt and uncle in Indiana. We go for walks or go swimming because Carl loves to swim. Carl will also pet Andy for hours, so I have to sometimes remind him not to pet so long lest the fur be worn off. And Wyrme will take long naps purring in his lap while Carl beams with happiness.

After finding out about Carl, I went on a quest to find others in my family and discovered some at different dimensional stations, much like you would visit a relative on earth who happens to live in another country. Belief systems, life experiences, and types of awareness determine which dimensional station one finds oneself in. My mom's dad passed four months before I did. He does not think the way I do, and therefore his experiences are different from mine, but when I came to visit him at level twelve he had no problem recognizing me, and he shouted out a big "Hello, Galen!" Through him I learned a lot about the Henderson side of my family, but also I have found friends, teachers, and even an alternate mother with whom I had an agreement. She, like Carl, is a family member who was not in my physical family; she would have raised me by herself, but then I would never have known my father. Because that wasn't what my dad or I wanted, he never met this woman on earth, and the agreement was dropped.

☙☙ ☙☙ ☙☙

Editor's note: For a moment I had some regret that Carl could not have been in my family, but I reminded myself that between moments of choice and the subconscious promptings that go with that, there is the flexibility of soul and spirit. Ultimately, I have to believe that the path we followed was exactly what needed to occur and precisely the one that served my soul, Galen's soul, and even Carl's soul. So it seems Carl's soul placed him in a more innocent time to experience the love and support of a family and then removed him before his own innocence was lost.

When I asked Galen why Carl had not matured on a personal level in half a century, the answer I received was that his maturation took place on an energetic level, which Galen experienced when Carl held his hand. At Galen's dimensional station one can shift one's appearance, but this is not taught at Carl's dimensional station. The mind-expanding sci-fi quality of level twenty-one that gives one the opportunity to work with these energies is not part of level seventeen. Because Carl's world was small on earth, his personality did not have the foundation to integrate all that he had been learning. Even so, Carl was able to find Galen, travel, and copy Galen's outfit and animal companions. According to Galen, Carl is now learning what can be done on level twenty-one and doing quite well.

Although Galen has pointed out that his passing served on numerous levels, many times he still questioned what happened to him. When Carl showed up in Galen's afterlife, Galen was still looking at why he had needed to leave in the way he did and Carl gave him another piece of the puzzle—all the agreements the soul makes even before one is born—which helped Galen better understand why he left earth.

We are not as stuck on the path we find ourselves on as we might think. If the soul has predesigned multiple probabilities, then as long as one is breathing, one need only decide to have a different experience and act on it.

Regarding Galen's maternal grandfather, a kind, almost child-like man, he was plagued by the ravages of diabetes and a precipitous fall into dementia throughout his last years. Unexpectedly, Galen was able to link me to him since Mr. Henderson was as interested in talking to me as I was with him. Like playing telephone, I sent out an exaggerated "Hello, Mr. Henderson," unsure what the reception would be like at his end.

He lamented that no one from his family on earth had spoken to him and he still wasn't sure where he was. "No one has talked to me. No one has told me," he moaned. I inferred that some portion of his personality was still shaking off his deep plunge into dementia, which had left him with little awareness of his passing.

He listened intently to what I had to say, as we had always respected each other. I gently told him his heart had given out because of his diabetes and that there was no need for concern as everyone knew. He asked me if that included his wife, apparently unaware that she had divorced him to marry a high school friend in his last years—but no way I was going to tell him that. He thanked me and gave a heartfelt "huh" of acceptance, as if I had added a missing piece of a puzzle.

It seems Mr. Henderson was demonstrating what happens when appropriate good-byes are not said, especially when the person doesn't know that he is passing. By contrast Galen, who was unchallenged in these ways, has the gift of understanding what happened to his body as he moved out of it. Galen chose to let his body go without fear or confusion, although in the moment he was not fully conscious of this decision. I found with Mr. Henderson that it takes only a moment of connection to ignite the missing awareness. All I had to do was put the explanation out there with my intention and not worry about whether the message was received or understood.

CHAPTER 11

Hair of the Wyrme

Carl has a tendency to be a little on the obsessive side, focusing intensely on whatever is in front of him—and thus demonstrating capacities beyond the scope of an average eight-year-old in much the same way that Andy has proved to be far more than a dog. One day when we were sitting on my rock along with Wyrme, Carl looked at Wyrme very intently, more so than usual. He would stare from one side of the rock then walk around to the other side and stare again.

After he had repeated this action several times, I asked, "What are you doing, Carl?"

"There is something different about Wyrme," he answered, concentrating on a particular spot on Wyrme's back.

It was hard for me to see what Carl was looking at because Wyrme was attached to my rock and to me at the same time. There is a certain technique for picking up Wyrme, because it can stick to whatever it is connected to if it doesn't want to let go, and therefore it can't be scooped up like a puppy or a kitten. It can most easily be picked up when curled into a fuzzy ball, so I asked Wyrme to compress. When it did, Carl became upset that whatever he had been looking at was gone. Andy started barking at Carl's whining, leading to quite a scene. When Carl settled down, I asked him what he had seen.

"I could see the stars in Wyrme's fuzz," he answered, excitedly.

I had never seen stars in Wyrme's fur, so I had Wyrme uncurl itself on Carl. Bending down to examine Wyrme, I saw nothing but the usual hairy fuzz. Then I walked to the other side of the rock, where the sunlight was streaming across more fully, and could see shiny beads like dewdrops on some of the hair.

"Can you see the stars?" Carl asked, eager for me to experience what had captivated him. "Can you see it?"

"I see tiny drops of moisture but nothing else," I answered.

Looking impatient, Carl suddenly plucked a single hair from Wyrme. Horrified, I took a couple of steps back, unsure how Wyrme would react. No one had ever taken anything from it before, and it responded immediately by contracting into a compacted fuzz ball, which started to roll off the rock until I scooped it up and put it into my pocket.

"Look at it through the sunlight," Carl urged.

Carl thrust the tiny hair at my face, and I held it up to the sun. I had never examined Wyrme's fur this closely before. It had a thin shaft that resembled that of a feather, but unlike a feather, Wyrme's hair had micro fuzz coming off the shaft. By focusing in as if I were traveling through a portal, I was able to make out small rainbow-colored prism-like images on the surface of the droplets. Then I saw something that nearly caused me to drop the hair. What I first thought was just some iridescence on the surface of the droplets were tiny Wyrmes somersaulting their way across the surface! It was like looking at a droplet of water under a microscope in biology class and seeing little one-celled organisms traveling through it.

Amazed, I sat back down on the rock and asked Carl, "How did you see this?"

"I saw little light beams and wanted to know where they were coming from," he answered.

I had never seen light beams coming off of Wyrme, but I knew Carl perceived things differently. Even though it seemed like I was running to my teacher almost every other day with questions, I had no choice but to return now, once again.

"I think I may have come to understand something about Wyrme," I said to my teacher as I very carefully handed Wyrme to him. "Look at it closely through light."

As my teacher held it up toward the light coming through his study window, I asked, "Do you see Wyrmes?"

"No."

"Keep looking," I urged, enjoying the idea of teaching my teacher.

Many minutes went by and then a look of surprise swept across his face, which delighted me because rarely did I see my teacher express emotion. He sat in an armchair, deep in thought, and then finally said, "I believe this creature is a hologram and that, when necessary, it reproduces itself holographically. It is likely we could take this hair and grow another Wyrme with it, if that were its destiny."

I remembered he had used a similar explanation when describing the silver cups, but I wasn't sure exactly what he had meant, because to me a hologram is a 3-D image that changes spatial orientation as you look at it from different angles. I was also trying to understand what he meant by the word destiny in this context. Still, excited by the thought of another fantastic creature, I blurted out, "Let's see if we can grow another one now!"

"No, it is not our choice to make," my teacher stressed. He explained that to grow a Wyrme from a hair removed without permission might upset the delicate balance in the universe of these rare creatures. "Its very nature requires that it be allowed to choose when it appears and when it does not," he added. My teacher then returned the hair to me, which I very carefully put back onto Wyrme, pleased that it adhered and hoping the many proto-Wyrmes living on that hair were not harmed.

Feeling a little embarrassed that I had let desire overtake me, I asked my teacher to explain what a hologram was.

"There are pieces of wholeness in the universe that work together to manifest physically, whether beings or planets. Nothing in the universe is really separate from anything else, and so every part of the universe is an important piece to another part. To have a being be a holographic image unto itself and to be able to physically see that wholeness in its very nature is indeed a magical thing. Just from one tiny hair, Wyrme can replicate itself over and over."

"Maybe there is only one Wyrme, and all others are just reflections of it," I said.

"Very much like Source and soul," my teacher added. "I have always believed there was a representation of this relationship somewhere in the universe, and Wyrme may be a representation of Source that re-creates itself to have experience and connect to others."

It was very interesting to watch my teacher ponder the possibilities and arrive at a new understanding rather than just stating something he had known about before. I still don't know what Wyrme is exactly, but I am glad to know that as long as there is even a minuscule part that represents the whole, then it will never be lost due to misuse or overuse. My thoughts drifted back to earth, where I knew the atmosphere was in a precarious balance, inching closer and closer to an event that could take away much of the life now present on it. I suspected the planet would survive but the life that was on it now would need to re-create itself.

At my dimensional station, everyone comprehends the interconnectedness of everything, and how all aspects of life integrate into the wholeness. If I could appear on earth, this is the message I would deliver: "Everything is so deeply connected to everything else that if we create an imbalance the whole of life suffers. This is a universal law and truth." I have talked to my teacher about the imbalance now occurring on earth, and he has told me that it means the current earth inhabitants will have to be replaced by a different experience, though the earth itself will continue to evolve. Imbalance creates another kind of balance.

Despite being in "heaven," earth experience remains of great concern to me because it affects the choices I have. Should I want to return to earth for another human experience, it may not be possible if earth humans no longer exist. Clearly, the unconscious path humankind is on affects far more than the earth, as is reflected in the lesson of Carl, whose life options were altered because certain choices couldn't align, requiring Carl's soul to make other choices. Everything we do affects everything else where one part holds the key to another.

◎ ◎ ◎

Editor's note: This is a spectacularly beautiful planet, and it is a privilege to be here even if for me the experience has been bittersweet. The commingling of illusion and reality— or what we perceive as reality—is the experience, making the earth an incredible school. Galen told me it is not his intention to be critical, but only to report that choices made do limit the options available to those who would want to return to earth.

As very few people on earth understand the difference between want and need, much of what is taking place here is out of balance. Wanting something unconsciously without needing it or understanding the full impact of our desire is out of balance. Furthermore, those who do not understand the interrelatedness of everything and the delicate balance of environmental factors are likely to keep causing imbalances that have, an increasingly negative impact on earthly life. It's troublesome that the ongoing destruction of the biosphere is in the hands of a greedy few who have no idea, in their blind arrogance, that there is a critical point from which there will be no turning back.

We have let others control our minds and our bodies, but no one can control our souls, so as a result of polarity there is always a battle raging here on earth. And while we can't eradicate polarity, we can choose to modulate it, preventing it from becoming too extreme. If we continue to act out of blindness and illusion, however, we are likely to exterminate one another. The universe will still have humans; it just won't have earthlings.

Choice is the most powerful thing on earth. For example, we allow energy to be produced from coal-fire power plants even though they release greenhouse gases and spew mercury into the land, sea, and air. Those who control this industry refuse to change their ways, though they could choose instead to regulate it. Although Galen lives in a dimension that does not use polarity as a teaching tool, it still ultimately affects his choices. You can take the human out of polarity, but you can't take polarity out of the human. Ultimately the nature of being human and the society Galen came from can obscure the human potential to exercise sane choice. By contrast, Galen quickly understood that his desire to see more replicas of Wyrme would have thrown reality itself out of balance and that another choice was available to him. It is the lack of such recognition, the difference between want and need, that is causing events on earth to be so out of balance.

CHAPTER 12

There and Back Again

I have great love for the earth. I cherish the people who live on it and the animals that walk, perch, and swim on it. Many of the scenes I create are the beautiful earth vistas I remember, unlike some of my friends here who create fantastical scenes of alien environments. Not only do I tend to be a little more traditional and stick with the familiar, but also I get very emotional while thinking about the planet I love so much. Like many of the ancient ones, I see earth as the mother out of whose matrix the spring of survival flows.

One particular day I had been thinking a lot about my earth life and suddenly felt a tremendous longing—a type of loneliness or emptiness, as if something were missing. When I first came in, I would have this sort of feeling often, but it was strange to have it now, especially since everything here allows me to create a strong foundation of emotional comfort. I wondered if the longing and emptiness meant someone in my earth family was moving to this side. I checked in to see what was going on with my dad, and everything looked fine as far as I could tell. I had heard others mention that when a member of their family was coming over from the other side they would get a message, and their teachers might even come for them if it was appropriate for them to be among those relatives the individual expected to see. But I had no sense of urgency or any visit from my teacher.

Troubled by my feeling of longing, I asked Andy to lie down beside me and pulled a purring Wyrme out of my pocket. I had a deep desire to speak to each member of my family. I thought about how much I loved my grandmother and how she would look at me with admiration, which always made me feel special. I thought about my mother and remembered her beautiful profile as I watched her look off into the distance or pet a dog, just as I was doing with Andy. I thought about conversations with my dad, his jokes, and quiet moments in which he expressed his enthusiasm for me to learn and experience new things. I loved the curiosity he evoked in me.

After watching the sunset, I went back to my house to sleep. More often than not I would sleep under the stars, but other times I felt like sleeping in a bed, and this was one of them. I wanted to feel comfortable, human, and part of a family. Dream-like experiences happen here while one is awake, so there is no need to sleep to have a conversation with oneself, which is often exactly what dreams are. I tucked a pillow under my head, and felt like I actually did fall asleep and start to dream. In this dream state, I found myself in a very long, arched hallway resembling those in Disneyland's Toontown and illuminated by multicol-ored, surreal-looking lights on the walls. I could hear someone banging on a door at the other end of the hallway and crying to be let in. I could feel Andy and Wyrme trying to alert me to something, yet I could not wake up, for some force seemed to be keeping me there.

I waited in this surreal hallway for a very long time. Then the door down at the other end crashed open and I could hear big foot-steps, like those of someone in heavy boots bounding toward me.

But the hallway was so long and the lighting so weird that I couldn't make out who it was. I could still hear the sounds of a person crying out and I was getting very anxious as I pictured a big cartoon lumberjack speeding toward me. Finally, I was able to make out that the figure was my father, which frightened me because I thought he had died on earth, although I had witnessed people crossing over many times and this was not usually the way it happened.

I jumped into the center of the hallway as my father—half cartoon, half human—closed the distance between us, becoming increasingly more human while doing so. He appeared to have a very powerful intention to come in through this hallway. His eyes widened and tears streamed down as he reached forward to touch me.

"Galen, I found you! Come here!" he cried.

Somehow my father must have discovered a portal and planned to cross over this way to live with me, but that is not how it is done. I didn't have a good feeling about the situation, as I did not know what would happen to his earth life or his earth body if he persisted and feared that he might get trapped in this hallway like the people in the windows.

"It is not time. You cannot see me this way. I promise that you and I will talk very soon, and that we will be together. But it can't be at this moment," I warned.

Then, before he could say anything else, I pushed his chest so hard it propelled him back down the hallway, and I could hear crashing as he fell through the doorway at the far end. I literally gave him an Almighty shove and even now I wonder if I had to push so hard. It was then that I realized the emptiness I'd been feeling was the fear he would have been trapped in this strange hallway, but the fear had not been mine.

Suddenly, I sat up in bed. My body was shaking and perspiration ran down my face. Andy was nudging my arm, and Wyrme was scampering around my body. I sat at the edge of my bed for a while collecting myself. As the dream had been so disorienting, it felt like I had to take stock of every finger and toe to make sure I was all there, but fortunately the feeling of emptiness was now gone.

By morning, everything seemed normal, with nothing in my environment even hinting at what had occurred. I decided to ask my teacher what had happened and then attend whatever class was being offered that day.

When I entered my teacher's study, he saw in my face that something was amiss and asked, "Galen, what is happening for you?"

I explained my experiences of the day before, from my feelings of emptiness to my dream state in which I encountered my father in the surreal hallway. He listened intently, as my confusion about what had occurred was evident.

"I didn't think it was possible to dream in this dimension," I said.

"No, one does not usually dream here, although it is not impossible if one really needs to be in a place of subconscious connection. This is what Matthew had to do to have that initial conversation with you when everything about this dimension was new to you. So there are times when one has to move into a subconscious dream space because there is a message that needs to be given." My teacher went on to explain that I had been preparing myself for this event, and while it didn't look real, rarely does subconscious energy appear to be real. He told me my father missed me so much he would do anything to witness me being here and say what he needed to tell me.

"Because the bond between you two is so strong, and because you share so much energetically with each other, he literally crossed over into this dimension using a subconscious portal," my teacher explained.

"I feared that if I did not stop him he would no longer be the person he was, so I had to push him out the portal so he could find his way back to his life," I explained.

My teacher went on to say that my dad had such a strong desire and need to connect with me that we actually touched in that space. I realized this was true even though I cannot create the exact feeling of my father's hand on my shoulder or the vibration of his voice because we are in different dimensions.

"You did save his life, and not just his earth life. I assure you that you will have a conversation with your father, but in a different way. Your father was literally touched by someone from this dimension who loves him dearly, and his heart will never be the same."

"What do you mean about saving his life?" I asked, still hoping to understand more.

"That subconscious portal led right into an antimatter dimension, and had he continued on, all the experience and wisdom he had gained as Ken and everything he held as part of a spiritual lineage would have been lost forever—and he would have dissipated along with a great part of that lineage. For the good of all, his soul made sure you were there to save his life and keep him on his path. That was why you couldn't wake up. You were made a guardian, to keep whatever came down that hallway from passing through—in this case, a grieving father who wanted nothing more than to see his son. Nothing else mattered to him; that is how strong the love is. It was a very intense moment of choice, because this was not about him being in one dimension or the other, but about him not being at all. This would have taken away a piece of his soul's lineage and made a big hole in the side of his cup."

"Vaporized!" I said.

"Not meaning to ascribe emotion to the soul, which is neutral, I'd say that your father's soul did not want to lose him and all the richness that he would add to its experience. In short, losing that lineage would not have served the highest good for all."

"My father has saved me many times, so I was glad I could be in the right place at the right time to save him," I said.

"And as you both met, you both changed," my teacher replied.

I flashed on when I was a toddler, barely able to walk, and thought I could go down a staircase in our home just like my father had done ahead of me, but instead I tumbled down. Out of nowhere, my father appeared and caught my head with his right hand just before my skull would have smashed into the baseboard near the bottom of the staircase. If he had not shown up at that moment, the damage to my head would likely have been too severe for me to survive. In a sense, because I was drawn to stand in the hallway he broke into, I returned the favor, but ironically the intuition and love that led me to save him resulted not in a gentle hand cradling his head but in a ferocious push that sent him crashing.

The experience with my father affected me for quite a while as I pondered how strong the will is in beings that incarnate in physical matter. They need to have a lot of power because the human body is a perpetual motion machine that requires willpower. It was that force of willpower that created the experience for my father. The challenge, it seems, is to balance will with guidance of the heart.

℗℗ ℗℗ ℗℗

Editor's note: The events Galen speaks of also had a profound impact on me, both physically and emotionally. With regard to Galen's experience as a toddler in our Altadena, California, home, no sooner had I entered the kitchen after going down the staircase than I did an immediate 180-degree turn at full speed to reach the bottom of the stairs because I had a feeling I needed to be there immediately. Galen had already tumbled halfway down the stairs, and without having time to think about it I put my right hand where his head would hit the baseboard molding. Miraculously his head landed exactly where I had placed my palm to catch it. In that moment I intuitively did what was in the best interest of all. In that moment, there was no separation, and the choice to listen or not listen to my intuition became the simple act of doing.

My little visit to the other side occurred in mid-June 2009, a couple of days before what would have been Galen's eighteenth birthday. I wanted so much to talk to him that I wrote the following journal entry, which reveals my state of mind just hours before I tried to cross over:

> I do not know what to do with that part of my psyche—the part that had the responsibility to protect Galen and see him into adulthood—for it feels like a failed charm, a little like the charm put on Harry Potter's aunt and uncle's house on Privot Drive, where nothing "evil" could touch Harry if he remained there until his seventeenth birthday. I almost got him there, but he left the house at Privot Drive before he was seventeen.
>
> Perhaps my now adult son is rolling his eyes at what I just said. Truly my efforts here are not driven by guilt; if anything, they are driven by a search for my own relevance.
>
> I was relieved when I heard that my very young son would pick up where my teachings left off—that he would be a philosopher or scientist—but I had yet to even begin my teachings. I remember almost walking on air after that conversation because I had just been given assurance my son would make it into adulthood and pick up the mantle of the teaching I was to be doing. Can a father ask for more than that? It was never my intention that Galen follow in my footsteps. I simply wanted him to be free to follow his own path, and it appears he has done that. What a legacy to leave to a world that so desperately needs truth tellers and truth seekers, and Galen is certainly that. For me, there is no separation between being Galen's father and my own relevance on this planet. I have no desire to continue being a stranger on this strange planet unless I am in a conscious relationship with

my son and of service to him and the fabric of life. It is asking a lot to be a bridge between worlds, but I have been through a great deal and now live a life that is more like a sci-fi movie, and not a particularly good one.

There is a saying that before the eyes can see they must be incapable of tears. I doubt my eyes will ever be incapable of tears.

I know Galen's new life is as full and rich as any he could have had on earth, if not more so. However, the sad fact is earthlings don't see it that way—they, with the exception of a rare Joan of Arc or a Prince Siddhartha, don't have conscious awareness or access to this other realm except perhaps in a fleeting dream or in the very last moments of their own incarnation. The other side is a never-never land to all but a select few. So here I am trying to be Peter Pan looking for a lost boy who is now an adult, which makes being short on fairy dust all the more poignant as I want very much to stand in his presence and hold him to my chest.

I am happy for you, my adult son—and as much as I loved all the various stages of your growth, even the little fellow I had to push up and down the streets looking for his mom, I had long waited to see you emerge as an adult. It truly was the adult Galen I was looking forward to knowing; we are just going to have to find this other way, and I have been trying and trying. I wish you all the best on this, the eighteenth anniversary of your birth, and hope my personality is able to talk with you soon.

When I wrote this, I had no idea I was hours away from going to never-never land myself. I had a pleasant dinner, sitting next to a window that gave me a nice view of individuals tending their boats outside the San Diego hotel where I was staying. As I returned to my room I was in an unusual emotional space, not depressed but fed-up so that if given half a chance, I would have stopped the world and gotten off.

During the night, I recall being in a trance-like state, with just enough of me present to execute the basic moves of getting out of bed to use the bathroom. But in doing this I tore the skin off almost the whole bottom of one toe pad. The reason I had to use the bathroom at all was because I had already found the portal—something called the Indigo Portal, which has yet to be integrated with the earth plane except to serve the purpose of providing a highway for souls traveling to and from the earth—so my body, thinking it was about to die, was preparing to evacuate. From the bloody footprints I left in the bathroom, I could tell I had made it as far as the door before I left through the portal, or lost consciousness. It seems as if I thought I could just take my physical body with me, but that obviously can't happen. Why or how I found the portal is not clear to me, but having found it, my body reacted accordingly, as if it expected death to occur, and it wasn't that far off the mark.

When I finally opened my eyes again while lying facedown on the floor, it was obvious that something untoward had taken place. My right foot was still on the tile on the bathroom floor, in a puddle of dried blood, making me think I had been passed out for at least an hour. My face was smashed into the carpet with an open-compound fracture to my nasal septum. I picked myself up and collapsed on the bed, not sure who I was other than Galen's father.

After a few moments, I remembered that Galen was not on earth. As this was an unpleasant emotional moment, I passed out again. I regained consciousness about two hours later, with enough of my memory restored to know where I was and that I had to testify as an expert witness about something in court in a few hours, which seemed unlikely, given my confusion. I called a physician friend who was staying at the same hotel to let him know I had been in some kind of accident. He arrived immediately, and we both tried to figure out what had happened.

We talked about whether I should be seen in an ER, but as I gained more clarity over the next hour, I said what I needed was hyperbaric oxygen and a good plastic surgeon, for besides my nose I had bitten completely through my upper lip. I felt present enough to testify despite the occasional drip of blood from my lip, but my injury was well hidden by my thick mustache, so I took a shower and got dressed.

After my testimony, I was driven to a hyperbaric oxygen chamber, then I flew back to Santa Fe, where I received more hyperbaric oxygen treatments and underwent surgery. It took weeks for me to adjust, as if I were trying to get used to being in an earth body. About a month later, my vision began to improve to the point where I no longer needed to wear my usual glasses. Perhaps this was a consolation prize from my visit to the other side, given I now have a lifelong scar on my upper lip and a nose that will never be the same.

Eventually, I did remember something about this trip—what it felt like to stand between an antimatter dimension and our matter dimension. In that place between universes, the level of despair was so intense I knew my psyche would have to surrender to it, and in so doing I would disintegrate after a finite period. Somehow I survived standing between the antimatter and matter dimensions, for had I not I would have been dead by the time my face hit the floor in San Diego. Apparently, or so I was told, my soul altered the path it was using to experience the earth dimension and, in service to all and to self, stood at a portal where one universe joins another. Had I continued down that hallway, not only would my persona have disintegrated but the spiritual lineage my soul had invested in the Ken incarnation would have disappeared, as Galen explained. Galen saved me from this fate but reminded me that avoiding antimatter universes was not the take-home message of our encounter.

CHAPTER 13

Earth Ambassador Brock

From the lectures I have attended here, I've learned there was a time when a more open exchange existed between the earth and my dimension, and as a result the human experience was more open and whole. The human mind and spirit, it is said, were so closely connected that little miracles were seen and acknowledged every day. Today, it is almost as if humans have forgotten how to see little miracles in everything.

In many ways, my dimension and the earth dimension are parallel. Although earth humans live in a world of polarity and I do not, the same emotions, the same trust in intuition, and the same perceptive understandings are available—so much so that one does not need to pass out of a material body to gain the knowledge available here. Still, it is impossible to produce a pink dragon out of thin air on earth, whereas one can definitely do so here.

On one occasion, I wandered the halls wondering which lecture to sit in on. I walked into seven different classrooms and had to leave because I got the message "No, there is something else." On my eighth try I sat down in the center of an empty room with chalkboards on all four sides. The features of this classroom were not as solid as others I had seen. For instance, the chairs were semitranslucent, so that as I sat on one I thought I might fall through it. Soon five students, all earthlings, began to file in, and I could see the hesitation in their expressions as they sensed the unusual feeling in the room and sat down on the opalescent chairs. Everyone was looking at each other without speaking when suddenly the room began to vibrate as if in response to a small earthquake. The students scrambled to hold on to their desks and remain seated as a being with no form I had ever seen before glided into the classroom on a misty cloud resembling the fog of dry ice. Its body was egg shaped, and brilliant orange hair trailed down the sides. Three pink appendages emerged from asymmetrical places—not so much tentacles but stalks that had pad sensors or feelers on them. It took all I had in me not to laugh because this being looked like the Addams family's Cousin Itt gone bad.

As I pondered whether this was a teacher or someone creating an image as a prank, the being finally took a seat in the back, somehow morphing into the right shape to sit on a chair designed for humanoids. Soon the teacher arrived—a human-looking man with broad shoulders who made everyone feel comfortable, like a favorite uncle. He had us introduce ourselves by name. When he looked at the unusual being, nothing was said and yet the teacher replied, "Thank you very much." The other six of us all looked like we had missed something, but the teacher called our attention to the front and began his lesson.

The lecture was about the nature of will. The teacher explained that the will does not impact things in a direct linear way, but indirectly more in the manner of how a pebble dropped into a still pond causes ripples to radiate outward in concentric circles. Such a use of will is more efficient than pushing will forward in a linear fashion and tends to balance energy as it expands outward. Further, he said that free choice is not available in every dimension but that the human mind assumes any dimension lacking free choice is like a prison. Free will, however, is not synonymous with free choice, he noted. Free will is about the right use of choice. When one aligns oneself with the right use of choice, one gains access to a unifying field of reality as opposed to a polarized field of reality.

While the teacher spoke, a shuffle could occasionally be heard at the back of the room, as if the mysterious being was adjusting itself in its chair. The teacher would look in its direction, nod his head, and say, "Yes, that is right," indicating there had been some type of telepathic exchange between him and the unusual student.

Eventually unable to stand the suspense anymore, I raised my hand. "I'm sorry, but I just have to understand something," I said. "Are you and the person in the back talking?"

"Yes, absolutely," answered the teacher.

"I'm not hearing anything. Does anyone else hear anything?" I asked. The students all shook their heads.

The teacher said, "Okay, if you all want to hear what is being said, that is fine."

I felt an odd popping in my ears, followed by a dulcet voice that filled the air and reverberated like a crystal bell—the most beautiful voice I had ever heard. I don't know how the unusual being was producing the sound because I could see no mouth.

The teacher asked the being, "Would you like to introduce yourself?"

In the most soothing tone, the being said, "Hello, my name is Brock, and I am new around here."

Then Brock laughed pleasantly, and I found I was quite enamored of him, because his voice reminded me of the comforting energy of Wyrme. Brock acknowledged that it was unusual for him to be present at this dimensional station because of his origin and shape, but permission had been given for him to work here for a while before transitioning into a human experience in the next incarnation. I found it fascinating that one could choose to transition between such diverse life forms. Here was a being that on his home planet may not have required oxygen or water, or that may not have even been from the third dimension at all.

"I will be attending classes before I make my transition, and I apologize that I did not include everyone in the conversation, because I had to adjust my vibration in order to be heard."

Brock said hello and everyone said hello back. The teacher then asked the class to face forward so he could continue teaching. When class was over, I couldn't pass up the chance to get to know Brock a little better. I stood right behind him while he glided down the aisle, trailing some of the misty fog that was present underneath his body. As he approached the door, he hesitated, seemingly anxious about going out, and said, "I apologize, Galen. I am still getting used to this dimension, and I haven't completely learned how to create the correct vibration to move out of the classroom that was prepared for me. When I said I was new, I literally meant I just got here."

"Take your time," I replied. "If you don't mind, I would love to walk with you."

I wanted to help him find a way to be more comfortable in this dimension, so I told him that when I first arrived I was given a little silver cup and, not seeing one on him, asked him if he had also received one. "The silver cup holds one's past experiences," I explained to Brock. "And it helps you align yourself in this dimension."

"No, I did not receive a silver cup, but I did have several teachers meet me. My agreement is to come into this dimension and get a sense for being human, as well as brush up on universal laws and truths."

I sensed Brock was getting more anxious. "Not to worry," I assured him. "I am with you here and you don't need to be nervous about anything."

Outside I could see the green grass and blue sky, cocreated by the earth humans here since that is what we like to see. But as soon as he had stepped outside, Brock froze, unsure about how to proceed.

"I don't perceive anything. How are you moving in nothingness the way you are?" Brock asked.

"You don't see grass or trees?" I replied.

"I don't even know what you are talking about," Brock answered.

It was clear that Brock had no experience in human realms. I wondered how he had even received permission to come into this dimension without knowing what a blade of grass might look like, so I asked, "What is it like where you came from?"

"Everything is flat and misty, and there is only liquid beneath us. The light is very soft, and there isn't a lot of it," Brock answered.

"Okay, let's start from there. Just imagine that you are home." Brock did, and it seemed to calm him a bit.

"Why is it you want to be human, given that you have no experience or understanding of human life?" I then asked.

There was a long awkward pause before Brock replied, "It is my understanding that the more diverse one's experiences are the more one is able to relate to others and assist others."

He told me he had come from a family of ambassadors and that every one of them had to take on a very different experience in unfamiliar worlds and bridge those diverse energies. It was his intention to follow in his family's footsteps, to one day be a planetary ambassador, and this was his first step on that path. He had been granted special permission to come here because of the reputation of his family. He said he was still young compared to others of his kind, and this was his first experience in his current position.

"Is there any way I can help you become more comfortable?" I asked.

"You could explain to me what grass is, or a tree, or what blue is."

As I realized the challenge of explaining what a blade of grass is to someone who has no idea what a human eye can see, I could feel Wyrme stirring in my pocket, wanting to get out, so I pulled it out and held it in my palm while it unfolded. This caused Brock to do a double take as he could sense that Wyrme was very unusual.

"Where did this come from?" he asked, surprised. "Where did you meet this one?"

"It joined up with me while I was traveling through some portals. I call it Wyrme." I replied.

"Wyrme?" Brock asked.

"Well, that is my name for it. I have no idea what this little being's real name is."

Brock and Wyrme were fascinated by each other because of their similar energy. Wyrme, quite taken with Brock, wanted to stretch over to him, although it did draw back when its politeness protocol kicked in. After all, Brock had not extended an invitation, and Wyrme's infamous classroom incident had taught it to touch only when invited.

"Would it be okay if Wyrme touched you?" I asked.

After Brock said yes, something very unusual happened. Wyrme made contact with Brock, and as it planted the other end of its tubular structure across my chest in front of my heart, I immediately saw what reality looked like from Brock's perspective. Wyrme had created a bridge between our two worlds, which would explain why it had been so eager to come out of my pocket moments earlier.

"Brock, I can see what your world looks like!" I cried.

"I can see what you are standing on, too, Galen. Is that grass? Is that green?" he asked, with the exuberance of a young child.

Clearly, Wyrme was helping this new ambassador comprehend the human experience for the very first time. And Brock was thoroughly enjoying the experience. Suddenly he started to laugh, which sounded like bells ringing, and Wyrme began to purr, as the two reveled in each other's presence. I joined in the symphony of sound with my own laughter, making us a trio of merry creatures from opposite ends of the universe.

I was glad I had been able to help this being start experiencing what it feels like to be human. I wondered and worried about what would be in store for him when he incarnated on earth. I thought he might become a famous singer or orator whose voice centered, comforted, and unified people. I hoped that his unique appearance would not cause him to be taken away and secretly warehoused as some oddity until he expired, for then the world would never know him as he is—one of the most pleasant heart-filled, well-intentioned beings of service, who is admired for his work.

With Brock, I had found a way to assist. That has been a driving factor in my life, whether on earth or here. Always I have wondered, how can I help others?

❧ ❧ ❧

Editor's note: Brock probably was not from the dimension where Galen resides, and so there was a certain amount of adjusting that had to take place on both sides for Brock and Galen to understand each other's experience. It is not of great importance to label levels and layers of various realms because we have no way to understand what such labels mean. For instance, we on earth have agreed that we inhabit the third dimension; I have been told the dimensional station Galen has arbitrarily called level twenty-one is actually one level of the fifth dimension. All such designations lack meaning when we have no frame of reference.

CHAPTER 14

Portal to Earth

After our first encounter, Brock and I spent many hours exchanging together, with Wyrme as the bridge between us, and I felt like he had become a close friend. While sitting next to my favorite rock, Brock and I could travel around my world. I gave him a detailed overview of my life on earth—from the trails I loved to images of my father, my mother, my grandmother, my classmates, and the dogs I knew. He delighted in this education in human experience. To show him a more balanced view of the earth, I included uncomfortable images, such as acres of garbage, clear-cut forests, factory farms, and oil spills. I tried to remain neutral as I showed him these things, because I realized Brock had committed himself to coming to earth and in a sense I was acting as his earth guide. Still, I couldn't help feeling his love and excitement about the earth and about being a human. So I did want to be sure my review was filled with my enthusiasm for planet earth.

After Brock had gone home for the day, I pondered my own excitement about being human. Certainly at times I had felt my life was a bummer and I wasn't excited about being alive, and many days I could have expressed more joy and gratitude. I wondered where along the way I had lost excitement for the experiment of being alive on earth. From my current perspective, I was able to look at the gift of being human and feel grateful for free will and choice. Having the choice to be joyful is a gift regardless of one's circumstance.

Brock and I met many times, and Wyrme was always so happy to see him that as he approached from across the field it would stretch way out, almost like a child who wanted his mother to pick him up. Sometimes ambassadors help others look at things more clearly, and indeed, I now was looking at what it meant to be human on a deeper level. Given that earth is likely where I will incarnate again, Brock did his job quite well.

After going through the usual politeness protocol, I tried to get Wyrme to tell me what he saw in Brock. "Are you enjoying our time with Brock?" I asked.

"Oh yes, very much so. He is a really good fellow. I enjoy his company." Wyrme responded in its unrevealing polite banter that gave no clue about what it was thinking on another level.

There were also times when Brock took me to his watery and soft world, where I could feel the misty coolness on my skin, making it a complete sensory experience. Brock actually brought me to his home world to visit his family. When I met them I knew immediately I was in the presence of incredible beings; but I could not tell one member from another, as they were all hairy orange, and egg shaped, with no variation in color or shape among them. And when Brock introduced me to his father, mother, brother, sister, and his neighbors, I couldn't tell if they were looking at me or not.

After we exchanged greetings, Brock asked those who were present to sing for me. It was a little awkward, as I felt like this was going to be one of those moments when you visit people and they ask if you want to see their home movies or watch little Timmy play the tuba. I nudged Brock to let him know they really didn't have to do this, but Brock said, "You must experience this." The group of eight began to sing with no audible words but every imaginable tone one could ever hope to hear all blended in perfect harmony. These were the most incredible sounds I had ever heard either on earth or in the many other realms I'd visited, permeating me so completely they moved me to tears. Earth humans would have thought of these beings as angels singing.

After they finished, I stood in silent awe, but then Wyrme poked me to be polite, so I became present enough to utter, "Thank you. That was a great gift—very lovely."

When we came back, which was accomplished by Wyrme detaching, I said, "That was the most amazing thing I have ever heard. What was it?"

"This is what we do," Brock answered. "We are universal ambassadors, and we sing because music is a universal language. We are able to sing to councils, and we sing into disputes so that both sides can find balance. I cannot tell you exactly what they sang to you, but it was about the soul you possess and the great things that are ahead of you."

"Who does your family sit in counsel with?" I asked with heightened curiosity.

"Earth is not the only planet that utilizes polarity," Brock replied, "and humans are not the only beings who do battle, or destroy their own world. We are often sent to bring awareness to other troubled worlds, but have been selected for now to assist on earth."

I was again reminded that human life on earth was in trouble. The earth has been in conflict for much of human history, and it truly needed an ambassador to help bring sanity.

"I don't mean to imply that you are not up to the task, but why isn't a more experienced ambassador being sent?" I asked.

"In many ways, the earthling experience is still very young. And since I am very young I can match the vibration," Brock replied.

I understood what he was talking about because I knew that in my dimension experience takes place in certain octaves and frequencies. I postulated that massive waves of energy coming together and creating different tonal signatures provided the foundation for various realms and levels. I thought about how Carl had been able to come over to my level by integrating some of these frequencies.

Brock told me that it is very unusual when one of his kind is sent on a mission, and at such times a great deal of effort goes into aligning opportunities to make sure the mission is fulfilled. He told me it was no accident that we were brought together—that I was selected to befriend him because I had enough experience as a human to have my own observations and make my own decisions, but not so much experience to have lost interest in being human. The other deciding factor was that my companion Wyrme, as the being most similar to Brock at my dimensional station, could serve as a bridge between us, critical to establishing our connection.

Brock's species, as he called it, all came from one being. These holographic beings are assembled over time slowly and purposefully, just like stars, as they move through phases of compression, expansion, and a drawing in of materials. The original member of Brock's species was a sentient being able to reproduce itself, much like Wyrme can do. Even though both Brock and Wyrme are holographic beings, they have different functions—Wyrme functions as a bridge between individuals and dimensions, while Brock serves as an ambassador between groups of beings.

Wyrme is driven by curiosity. That doesn't make it self-serving, because Wyrme is generous, but it serves the curiosity of self, so there doesn't need to be an army of them; the curiosity is satisfied in that one unit. I feel like its pet at times, but it absolutely loves being with me because of all the action that goes on around me. Curiosity attracts the curious, it seems, and for now Wyrme is happy in this dimension. It has all its needs met and doesn't have to crawl around.

In contrast, there is a great need to have a whole family of ambassadors like Brock, whose singing can bring peace, their very reason for being. Brock's kin are eternal but not invincible, as the form they take can be killed in the third dimension, in which case the body vanishes because the material used to create it operates at a higher vibratory level than third-dimensional matter. From there, they reassemble themselves back in their home realm, manifesting as hairy orange eggs once again. There was one exception: a member of Brock's family was once caught in a cataclysmic event on a galactic scale and could not keep his form assembled. Although there have been no such events on earth, those occurring in other parts of the universe could cause a being like Brock to be blown apart so quickly the ability to reassemble would be lost—like what would have happened to my father if he had proceeded into the antimatter universe.

In another conversation I told Brock that my experiences with him had helped me better comprehend some of my earth experiences and receive confirmation that on a universal level there is a grand intelligence and rhythm at work, and that a succession of new information had been coming in that made sense to me, all since his family had sung to me. Then I thanked him for helping me gain these insights.

"You are most welcome, Galen. And I must tell you this is our last real meeting together as it is time for me to depart for earth. I can't thank you enough for what you have done to help me be more comfortable as a human. I will leave in the morning." Brock said this with a laugh, because he was practicing being in linear time. Then he added, "Will you meet me in the morning? I want you there when I leave."

"Absolutely!" I said, thinking how strange that Brock knew the timing of his parting. I had seen the comings and goings of many in and out of this dimension, but had never known one could be assigned a particular moment to leave. "Yes, I will be happy to be there."

"Please bring Wyrme, and would you also bring Andy? I would very much like to meet Andy before I go."

"Absolutely!" I said again. I had told Brock about Andy, though they had not yet met. I described how I could look into Andy's eyes and notice a being completely different from anything one would think sits in that skin.

The next morning was beautiful, with a perfect sunrise, birds singing, and the sky as blue as I could think it to be. I started walking toward my rock a little unsure because Brock didn't say where to meet him; nevertheless, I could see him on the hill, glowing in the morning sun, which had created a brilliant fuzzy orange aura around him, so magnified that I will never forget that stunning sight. I quickened my pace, concerned he was already in the process of leaving. I had Wyrme in my pocket and called out Andy's name, but he didn't appear. Turning my head back, I whistled across the field for him, but still I didn't see him.

Andy is a free will being who can come and go as he pleases. Hoping that I was not letting Brock down, I apologized about Andy's absence, then I asked why there were no teachers present, as normally a teacher will walk an individual toward the Hall of Cups en route to their passage to earth. "I don't see anyone here to take you to earth. Maybe it is because you don't have a cup. My understanding of this dimension may be limited by my human experience, but I thought beings had to go down a certain path toward the Hall of Cups, then their physical forms dissipate into energy and they are sent toward the vessel that will receive them—the womb of their next mother—as they set their cups back on the shelf," I said. "How will you be born? How will you arrive on earth?"

"Let me explain. I don't have a cup because I have not passed out of my body. My kind do not live or die in the way you have come to understand. We all began from one original being who was literally sung out into the atmosphere. When I come to earth, I will simply appear. I will be found as a baby and placed in an orphanage. I will have a mother and father who will feel a connection to me and raise me. I will follow the human cycle of growth, aging, dying. As long as possible, I will be an ambassador who will serve in the ways that are allowed. I will be love on earth. When I can do no more and it comes time to leave earth, I will dissipate—my body will not be found—and I will return to my family," said Brock.

I was surprised to learn that Brock was going to earth as a human—a disguise he would keep for his entire life there. I thought only humans came to be humans, and that one could only travel between dimensions by leaving their form behind. It was a real eye-opening moment to realize I was in the company of another eternal being.

I don't know if fuzz and hair is part of being eternal, but I could now see why Brock and Wyrme had an immediate connection and could work together so closely. Sure, humans were a curiosity to Wyrme with all their emotions, but Brock felt like a fellow being, someone more equal than a pet (like me).

"Have you figured out what you are going to look like on earth?" I asked.

"Oh yes, I have planned that well. I am definitely going to have orange hair," he remarked.

"You might want to keep it toned down," I said and laughed. "Bright orange hair will be seen as a little odd by your fellow humans."

With that, Brock began to vibrate, an energy I felt in my own body as well. As everything around us started to lose its form and become transparent, Brock emitted an intense brightness. Then I could hear Andy's bark as he ran up the hill, but to my surprise he ran past me and leaped toward Brock. While suspended in midair, Andy arced in slow motion into the space Brock had just occupied but which now was only a blinding white light. And then with a pop they were both gone. Only a lingering smell of ozone hung in the air, as if a lightning bolt had just fired through that space.

Taken by surprise, a part of me did not want to acknowledge that Andy had just accompanied Brock to earth. Andy was my best friend and the first being to teach me about appearances. The deep loss I felt following his departure, however, was mixed with a renewed hope for life on earth.

❀ ❀ ❀

Editor's note: On earth, two years and five months had gone by since Galen's crossing. But he had obtained many more years of experience if his sojourn there were converted into linear earth time. In fact, when these events were taking place, Galen considered himself to be well into his mid-twenties.

I was aware not only that Andy's departure was very sad for Galen but that it had actually just happened for Galen, so I wanted to say something fatherly to him. I told him that if there was such a thing as doing well in heaven by using one's time there being present and of service, then it seemed to me that he was doing well. Most humans have a deep desire to know their purpose or create one, because ultimately the human is a being of service, and to know one's purpose is to know one's spirit. Had Galen remained on earth, I am sure he would have become an important teacher one day, although it would have taken him a long time to figure out what he has come to understand in the blink of an eye in his current dimension.

Throughout his time there, Galen's love for his family and his eagerness to learn, two driving forces in his earth life, have prevailed. Apparently these are some of the energies we take with us to the other side. In a sense, nothing else matters.

CHAPTER 15

Miss Lavender's Lesson

The day after Brock and Andy left, I decided to attend class, hoping some of the wonderful offerings at school might help relieve my sadness. I looked down the posted list of classes, but nothing stood out for me. Aware that sometimes the body knows what the mind doesn't, I began to walk past classrooms to see if one drew me in amidst my condition of feeling numb and partly present. Sure enough, I was drawn to a classroom that was not one of my favorites, but I trusted the magnetic pull that took me there.

The back of the room was occupied by what looked like a tricked-out science lab, with unusual beakers and glass-like tubes that emitted puffs of smoke. The tubes reminded me of biology class on earth and creepy dissection exercises. Reluctantly, I entered the room, looked again at the array of tubes in back, and headed in the opposite direction, sitting as close as I could to the front. The room filled up rapidly, and soon hardly an empty seat was in sight, leading me to think we were in for a good class although I didn't know what the topic of the lecture was going to be.

Moments later, a very beautiful woman walked in wearing a traditional black teaching robe—not all the teachers wear robes, but I almost had the sense she wore it to be a little less distracting as she was quite stunning. Her lovely red hair was loosely pulled back, causing me to feel a palpable twinge in the pit of my stomach from the loss of my redheaded friend. I wondered if the class was so full because the other students were attracted to it by the beauty of this teacher rather than the subject matter. Hey, I may be dead, but I'm not *that* dead.

The teacher wrote her name on the board—"Miss Lavender"—turned around, and began her lecture on beauty and its effect on the chemistry of the emotional body. For a moment I wondered whether this was someone who made herself appear lovely but whose true appearance may have been completely different. My thoughts shifted when I realized her lecture wasn't about physical beauty but rather how that which is in balance opens the emotional body that proceeds to view the balance as beautiful. Miss Lavender went on to talk about how we look for balance in everything we see.

All I could think about was Brock. Even though Brock's appearance, by earth standards, was disturbingly odd, the balance he projected was beautiful and everything he did was beautiful. Even Wyrme, by earth standards, would look fake and only as attractive as a child's toy, but its use of balance to arouse curiosity did indeed make Wyrme attractive to the curious.

The gist of the lecture was about how the emotional body interprets the energy around it and how finding the balance in one's observations actually helps heal and align the physical earth body. A point well taken, I thought, but I don't have an earth body. Looking around the classroom, I noticed that all the students had a powder-blue glowing edge around their bodies. I held my arm out but didn't see a glow around my own body.

Having never seen this phenomenon before, I wondered if it was caused by the contents of one of those bubbling tubes or beakers, or if it was due to an energy field the teacher was emitting.

"Pay attention, eyes forward," Miss Lavender said, calling me to task for being so distracted.

I felt like I was in third grade again, but I snapped to. Yet as she continued to teach, my mind kept going back to Brock and Andy leaving without so much as a good-bye. The aloneness I felt kept welling up, and I could tell the teacher had her eye on me but didn't call me on it.

When she finished her lecture, many students came up to thank her and shake her hand. She, in turn, made an overt effort to connect physically with each one, either through a tap on the shoulder or a pat on the back. To every student I could hear her say something like, "Be strong" or "Be clear." I couldn't make out every little aphorism she bestowed, but was mesmerized by her ability to engage with each student.

Then she looked at me. "Galen, would you like to talk about something?"

I was feeling closed down, so I diverted my eyes to my desktop and didn't respond.

"I know you have gone through something big," she persisted. "Would you like to talk about it?"

Of course I wanted to talk about it. So I began to tell her about the wonderful friendship I had with Brock and how he opened me up emotionally, and how her lecture helped me understand this a little better, but still I was feeling the effect of his departure. "I have no idea what happened to my friend Andy either. I didn't get to say good-bye—just a sudden leap, and poof," I added.

Miss Lavender explained: "I understand you are still a student occupied with all the incredible opportunities that are here in this dimension. But if you back up and watch the rhythm of this dimension, you will notice comings and goings as busy as those on earth. There are times when one doesn't get to complete something before leaving—or so it appears to those who are left behind.

"You believed that Andy was not only your teacher but your companion, and you believed he would always be here with you. Andy has a very different agenda. Andy does not live in this dimension, nor is he part of your creation. You are clever enough to have already figured out that Andy was not who Andy appeared to be, nor was he even Andy, but rather something you both agreed you would work with to hold the teaching of friendship and connection. Andy is a sentient being and very aware of what he needs to do."

I was trying to find comfort in her words, but couldn't overcome my feelings. "Where did Andy go? What happened? Why didn't he let me know? Why didn't he see me the night before?" I blurted out.

When I finished venting my emotions, Miss Lavender looked at me calmly and said, "Andy had to return back to earth."

"Was it because of Brock—because Brock was going to live as a human for a while?"

"No, it had nothing to do with Brock, but it did have to do with the opportunity to use a portal that does not require the need to be conceived and born. Brock was going to simply arrive; his beginnings will always be a mystery. So Andy hitched a ride in this unusual portal, an event that had been planned all along. Andy has already taken over the body of another and will continue that life on for the individual. Such situations are very rare but they do occur."

I knew what Miss Lavender was talking about because my father had observed this taking place after the big tsunami at the end of 2004 hit the Indian coast. In dream, he had watched a twelve-year-old boy lose his life and then be placed in the body of a mentally impaired man more than twice his age—a "walk-in," he called it. The transition was very difficult emotionally, as it was not where this boy wanted to be and he felt his life had been stolen from him. But it did clear up a mystery for me about why there was more to Andy, with those eyes so clear, and why Andy was a teacher of appearances—because he didn't have his own appearance. Andy, it turns out, is a symbiote, a being that can merge with the material of another, without destroying that material, and accelerate the tenor of that life to help complete a task.

"He took that opportunity, in which he didn't have to be conceived or born, to occupy a human form on earth," Miss Lavender said.

I was a little dumbfounded because it had never occurred to me to think about what the being inside Andy—camouflaged as a dog—would do next, but I saw it happen with my own eyes. Although he held his station as a dog quite well, I experienced Andy in many ways, so I completely understood the likelihood of his moving back to earth as a walk-in I could accept that.

Miss Lavender told me that many humans relegate their souls and spirits to the back of the subconscious areas of their psyches, while their personalities play out an illusion of mind. So for the man whose body is now occupied by Andy, instead of having a personality play out an illusion of mind he will have a highly conscious being occupy that space, the being formerly known as Andy. She said it is not done often because a deep agreement is required and because the being in question must be able to influence, teach, and reflect. This is the opposite of the malevolent entities that occupy a space in individuals with severe addictions, destroying their lives as they feed off of their habits. Although the space is the same, when filled with an awareness of spirit and soul there is no way an undesirable occupant, whether illusory or parasitic, can enter.

"I still feel bad for not being able to introduce Andy and Brock," I told Miss Lavender.

"In a way they did meet, but Brock has an awareness of these opportunities, and he will be a teacher that elicits not only harmony but an awareness of the impossible, proving theories that many scientists on earth are still struggling with. Brock wanted to meet Andy because of the type of being Andy is. Just like he learned from you how to be a human, he was interested in knowing a symbiote. Awareness on earth is changing,"[1] she added, but didn't elaborate.

"Where did Andy go?" I asked her.

"There was a young man, about twenty-four years of age, in a coma from a skiing accident from which he would not have recovered. He has now woken up. Almost all his memories have gone to the back of his subconscious mind, but he still retains the basic skills of walking and talking, and shows a vague familiarity with his family. Before he was born, his soul and spirit had agreed that in case a situation like this arose, they would step aside and observe what would then become an extraordinary life of service and clarity. The life of that lovely young man affects many others around him, so it was important for it to be sustained—which is what the being formerly known as Andy does."

I thanked Miss Lavender for clearing up the mystery of Andy and what had occurred. Laughing to myself because Andy was no longer Andy, was never Andy, and yet would always be Andy to me, I still felt the loss.

"I have one more question for you, Miss Lavender," I said as I was about to exit the classroom. "Why did everyone in class radiate a blue glow?"

She laughed. "They are all returning back to earth.[2] Returning back in the usual fashion—conception, birth, and so on and so forth."

---

[1] There is an increasing awareness on earth that everything is connected, and nowhere is this understanding greater than in appreciating how one consciousness can merge with another.

[2] The subtle blue glow looks like a membrane and I was told there is an actual physical shift in the composition of a body belonging to someone who is close to returning to earth. The blue field of light is the mark of reincarnation when a body is actively preparing for the journey back by moving into an etheric form so it can merge with earth matter on the other side. I owe my ability to see this blue energy shift to Brock and his family, for their singing brought up my ability to understand subtle energy shifts.

That gave me pause. "Am I returning too?" I asked.

"No, not yet. You always have a choice, but I suspect you have much more to learn here first. Of course, returning back to earth does not require one to complete a certain course or obtain a particular understanding; although there is wisdom in doing so, things don't always happen that way. The soul respects free will and choice."

"So why was I drawn to this classroom?" I asked.

Miss Lavender laughed again and said, "Someone had to tell you who Andy was. Someone had to let you know that your friends didn't leave you and had been saying their good-byes all along. Andy loved you deeply. He stood faithfully as your teacher and friend. Andy didn't abandon you; he moved forward. Just as you will do, and have already done."[3] Then she gave me a wry smile.

I thanked her again and was grateful I had followed my instinct to sit down in that classroom. It did make me feel a bit better.

∞∞ ∞∞ ∞∞

Editor's note: Although dogs figured prominently in Galen's earth life and he had many dogs at his mom's house, at my house there was usually only Sprout. I first met Sprout in the summer of 2002, when a patient brought him into my waiting room and I overheard her saying she had just rescued him and named him Sprout because he sprouted out of nowhere, but she couldn't keep

---

[3]This comment refers to how much I have progressed since moving into this dimension, but also my path here has advanced beyond what would have been required to return back to earth. At times I long to go back, but I have a very specific goal to accomplish. When I do go back, I am told, I will have full conscious access to a great deal of what I have learned on this side.

him. I walked around him a couple of times and said he could stay. He has accompanied me to my clinic almost every day since then, and my patients call to him so they can pet him. I remember telling Galen over the phone that he had a new dog, and when he asked what he looked like, I said he looked like he jumped off the page of comic book or escaped from a circus. From the start I felt there was more than just a dog in there since he behaved unlike any of the dogs I had known.

Galen noted that Sprout's energy is similar to Andy's—not that he is a developed symbiote of Andy's caliber, but that he emits something more than basic dog awareness, is extremely comfortable with humans, and serves very well as a companion. Certainly, Sprout is more than just a lovable, well-behaved dog I never had to train; he's a wise soul that serves as protector, companion, and guardian, all masked in the body of a dog.

Galen said it was no accident that Sprout came into our family, and that Sprout knows when Galen connects with me because Sprout really loved Galen. I taught Galen that the animal kingdom holds the true nature of the earth experience and that animals are the ultimate teachers for understanding life on earth. It is not hard to imagine that many developed conscious beings may want to experience that role and participate with members of the animal kingdom, especially those having intimate contact with humans, such as a beloved dog, horse, bird, or cat. While it is certainly not the case for every dog or cat, it is the rule rather than the exception, and although few are as developed as an Andy, there are many more like Sprout.

The universe is teeming with developed conscious beings, and inhabiting the body of a beloved family pet can provide important learning opportunities, whether by working directly with a human being or as one's protector, teacher, or companion. Just imagining them utilizing the opportunities earth offers can cause us to stop and think about how we act toward our younger brothers, as Native Americans call members of the animal kingdom. Some may be our equals and others more than equals—that is, more highly developed conscious beings than we are. As humans, we are hosting many on this planet, and if appearances are as deceiving as they seem to be, it would behoove us all to demonstrate the utmost respect to all species.

While it is true that humans traditionally eat animals, when human societies were closely connected to nature they would bless and thank the spirits of the animals they had hunted and killed. On the other hand, being cruel to creatures we share the planet with does not reflect well on humankind, nor does it serve the animal kingdom. Treating animals cruelly or abusing them is frowned upon not out of judgment but because such actions benefit no one.

In fact, many humans respond to animals more openly than they do to fellow humans—they trust animals, love them, and bring them in close. It is known that animals can be tremendously therapeutic for those who feel lost or distanced from loved ones. The reason for this is that such animals are teachers on levels never imagined. The earth is a schoolhouse, and its teachers come in all shapes and sizes. We are never alone on this planet (a truth to both take great comfort in and celebrate.

Sprout

Epilogue

The day Andy left, I played over and over in my mind the arcing leap that took him away. Even now the scene remains vivid, including the ozone smell that lingered in the air. I sat down and stared into the spot from which Andy and Brock had disappeared. At first I wouldn't allow myself to completely acknowledge that Andy had left, though I had no choice but to admit he had definitely departed from that spot. I knew Andy wasn't a dog, but never did I think he would leave me. Sure, I would miss Brock and was sad about losing his friendship, but with Andy it was like one of my arms had been pulled off. Feeling such a deep sense of loss is a rare occurrence in my dimension but it does happen. I reminisced about Andy playing catch with me with a ball or stick, because he liked to do the usual dog things, and I regretted there would be no more of that.

Beyond the discovery that looks are deceiving, another lesson awaited me: that there is a purpose and reason behind everything that takes place. But for the next few days I just let the shock of Andy's departure overwhelm me. I continued to attend classes, sometimes running into familiar classmates or studying with a familiar teacher. One day just blended into the next until slowly I realized how much Andy had defined my existence in this dimension. I thought about my dogs on earth and how they had each occupied a space in my life, much like individuals who stand beside us can fill a need so that when they are no longer present they are very much missed.

Brock had opened me up to a whole new field of wisdom and understanding, a gift that has stayed with me. He introduced me to the idea of changing my perception by stilling my mind and body and moving into greater openness. Wyrme, when it stirred, was also lovely, curling itself around my neck and purring. But no one could bring forward the clear exchange of love I had with Andy. Those in our lives who hold space, I realized, also hold love—an epiphany that opened my heart.

I returned to my rock with a new awareness of how much space the feeling of love occupied in my world. Going within, I soon realized that the force most central to the matrix of the universe is love. I then understood, to my very core, that I would never feel alone again. It was a new sense of belonging and gratitude I could share with my family, Brock and his family, and Carl. Actually, I could share this new level of connection with anyone on my side of the universe. Here, while there are different choices than on earth and a wider field of opportunity in which to create, one still needs the essential connection that comes with feeling love.

I spent a great deal of time resting next to my rock listening to the slight purr of Wyrme, watching the clouds move across the sky, enjoying the green grass—not even thinking about how I was creating these things—and realizing that I was just being. Opening my awareness, I could see my whole childhood, from the moment I was conceived and decided to breathe in love, grow, and have a human life. I was able to trace my life all the way through to the present moment, and throughout I experienced the same feeling of connectedness I had when Brock's family sang to me. It was amazing that I could reproduce this feeling unassisted by anything outside of myself, and it was then that I knew I would never be alone again.

Before long, I sat up and decided to go find Carl. It felt right, at that moment, to just be with my little brother for a while.

Editor's note: Galen's peak experience of realizing he was part of the One and there was no separation between him and anything else, is the quintessential moment of becoming fully awakened to one's nature, one's true self. When this state is obtained in an earthly material body dedicated to service, Buddhists call it the way of the compassionate Buddha. Other religions have different names for this esoteric state that, once obtained, awakens us from our slumber and frees us from participating unconsciously in the everyday grind of life. The drive to be awake may be the main subconscious force creating awareness.

One of the biggest obstacles to becoming fully awake is the personality, which measures, compares, and judges. Its tools don't bring anything useful to the table of enlightenment, and yet one cannot just ignore the personality or walk away from it. In fact, the personality—or the ego structure connected to it—is often considered the final gate to move through in achieving enlightenment. At this gate the personality can become part of the wholeness, and thus become neutral. Being neutral does not mean having no emotion or thought; rather, it means that a shift of perspective has taken place in which everything is perceived as equal.

The challenge is accessing this perspective when the personality blocks it, for every individual is always in a state of awareness. Indeed, every sentient being on earth is in a state of awareness; the issue is connecting to that awareness, which can be found beyond reason or intellect.

In Galen's dimension, it seems the personality becomes neutral with far greater ease than it does on earth and may in fact explain what he was able to accomplish at his Bodhi rock, a comment not meant to detract from his accomplishment. His unusual experiences, which may be out of the ordinary even for his dimensional station, might be training him to become an assistant teacher lecturing in one of the classrooms—at least in the extension program. That is what I see in my dreams.

On earth one might wonder, why has knowledge of this other dimensional reality in which we will someday sojourn been, at best, shrouded in myth and fable and, at worst, distorted or obfuscated by religious dogma. If it were reclaimed from the annals of esoteric traditions or from the hands of those who seek to control humanity, we might have a more grounded appreciation of circumstances that await us in a continuation of consciousness beyond this material plane of existence, and we might take more responsibility for the way we conduct ourselves while on earth.

Generations ago, humankind depended on instinct for survival, and with that also came instinctual knowledge of such a realm. But no longer do we teach our children to rely on their instinct to survive in the physical world or to connect with their spirit or that of the earth, as if we even knew what to teach. As such, the ancient knowledge has been all but forgotten, perhaps in our desire to feel secure in large numbers. Paradoxically, however, in this trade-off we feel less safe because we have lost our access to inner guidance, should we really need it.

As centuries go by and humanity evolves into the age of the heart chakra, the knowledge that was once lost will hopefully find its place again within us, perhaps in humankind's more expansive hearts. And when it comes back, rejoined by the power of human instinct, it won't be there for survival, like it had to be for our ancestors, but rather for understanding that there is much more around us than meets the eye and that consciousness continues beyond our earth-given bodies. Fortunately, a memory of this expanded awareness is kept alive in the creation stories of indigenous people around the world and in the practices of their "wisdom keepers."

In a similar vein may *My Life after Life*, a project between father and son, help build upon this memory and thus contribute to a growing awareness of universal laws and truths. I am holding a space so that Galen can move forward, and he is holding a space so I can do the same. I believe in the probability of the impossible. And I'm sure all that really matters is a heart that can love unconditionally—the ultimate unstoppable force.

Acknowledgments

This book could not have been written without the connection provided me, the editor, by the trance medium Audrey Wrinkles. Without her dedication to holding a space so the guides that work with her could train me, explain my dreamtime experiences, bridge, translate, and validate, this book would not exist. They provided solace during the most difficult time of my life, and made sure I knew I did not walk alone.

I am grateful to Suzy Ward, who was there for me almost immediately after Galen passed, and of course, her son Matthew. Suzy introduced me to grief counselor and author Terri Daniel, who acted as my assistant editor.

I also owe a debt of thanks to several friends who allowed me to read each and every chapter to them, including Julie Gordon, Gail Fiverson, and Mattea Gonzales. Thanks also to Heather and Avery King, who endured listening to me read my journal before Galen even asked me to write down his book.

A special thanks to Paul Martin of the Search and Rescue Dog Association of Southern Scotland, whose dog Cairn was the model for the painting of Andy by Santa Fe artist Chris Kelly (see insert).

Lastly, a note of appreciation to Ellen Kleiner of Blessingway Authors' Services and all those she gathered in to help this book become real.

About the Author

Galen Stoller was in many respects an all-American kid. He liked going to theme parks and movies, visiting his grandparents, hamming it up at school, and hanging out with his friends. Steeped in the world of sci-fi/fantasy, he read the complete Harry Potter series, the Golden Compass/Dark Material series, and the Bartimaeus Trilogy. He also read the C.S. Lewis Narnia series over and over, except for the last book, in which all the protagonists were killed in a train accident—a volume he read once and never wanted to return to.

It was a train accident that would take Galen's earth life when he was sixteen years old. At the time, Galen was in eleventh grade at Desert Academy in Santa Fe, New Mexico, and starting to think about enrolling in college. An accomplished actor, he was about to perform the dual roles of Fagan and Bill Sikes in *Oliver!* He was an ethical vegetarian and helped train dogs for Assistance Dogs of the West. Because of this service, he was nominated posthumously for the 2008 Amy Biel Youth Spirit Award. Following the second anniversary of his passing, he asked his father to start writing *My Life after Life*, the first book in what he called the Death Walker series.

About the Editor

K Paul Stoller, MD, started his medical career as a pediatrician and was a Diplomat of the American Board of Pediatrics for over two decades. Previously, in the early 1970s, he was a University of California President's Undergraduate Fellow in the Health Sciences, working in the UCLA Department of Anesthesiology and volunteering at the since disbanded Parapsychology Lab at the UCLA Neuropsychiatric Institute. He matriculated at Penn State and then completed his postgraduate training at UCLA.

His first published works, papers on psychopharmacology, came to print before he entered medical school. During medical school, he was hired to do research for the Humane Society of the United States and became involved in an effort to prohibit the use of shelter dogs for medical experiments, which made him very unpopular in certain circles when he published an article entitled "Sewer Science and Pound Seizure" in the *International Journal for the Study of Animal Problems*. He was then invited to become a founding board member of the Humane Farming Association, and served as science editor for the *Animal's Voice Magazine*, where he was nominated for a Maggie Award.

In the mid-1990s, after a friend, head of Apple Computer's Advanced Technology Group, lapsed into a coma, Dr. Stoller began investigating hyperbaric medicine. Soon after, he started administering hyperbaric oxygen to brain-injured children and adults, including Iraqi vets and retired NFL players with traumatic brain injuries, also pioneering the use of this therapy for treating children with fetal alcohol syndrome. He is a Fellow of the American

College of Hyperbaric Medicine and has served as president of the International Hyperbaric Medical Association for almost a decade.

When his son was killed in a train accident in 2007, he discovered the effectiveness of the hormone oxytocin in treating pathological grief. Dr. Stoller has medical offices in Santa Fe, Sacramento, and San Francisco.